CITIZEN RACING

CITIZEN RACING
John Caldwell
Michael Brady

The Mountaineers/Seattle

THE MOUNTAINEERS: Organized 1906
" . . . to encourage a spirit of good
fellowship among all lovers of
outdoor life."

©1982 by John Caldwell and Michael Brady
All rights reserved

Published by The Mountaineers
715 Pike Street, Seattle, Washington 98101

Published simultaneously in Canada by Douglas & McIntyre, Ltd.
1615 Venables Street, Vancouver, British Columbia V5L 2H1

Book design by Marge Mueller
Illustrations by Odd R. Pettersen
Manufactured in the United States of America

Cover photo: Engadin Skimarathon Citizens' Race, Switzerland.
   (Photo by C. Filli, Celerina, Switzerland)

Title page photo: Meeri Bodelid, women's winner in the 1981 Vasaloppet.
   (Photo by Lars-Erik Klockner)

Library of Congress Cataloging in Publication Data

Caldwell, John H., 1928—
   Citizen racing.

   Bibliography: p.
   Includes index.
   1. Cross-country ski racing.   I. Brady,
M. Michael.   II. Title.
GV855.5.R33C34   1982   796.93   82-14382
ISBN 0-89886-041-5 (pbk.)

To Hep and Marianne — wives, citizen racers, and critics — without whose support this book would not have been written.

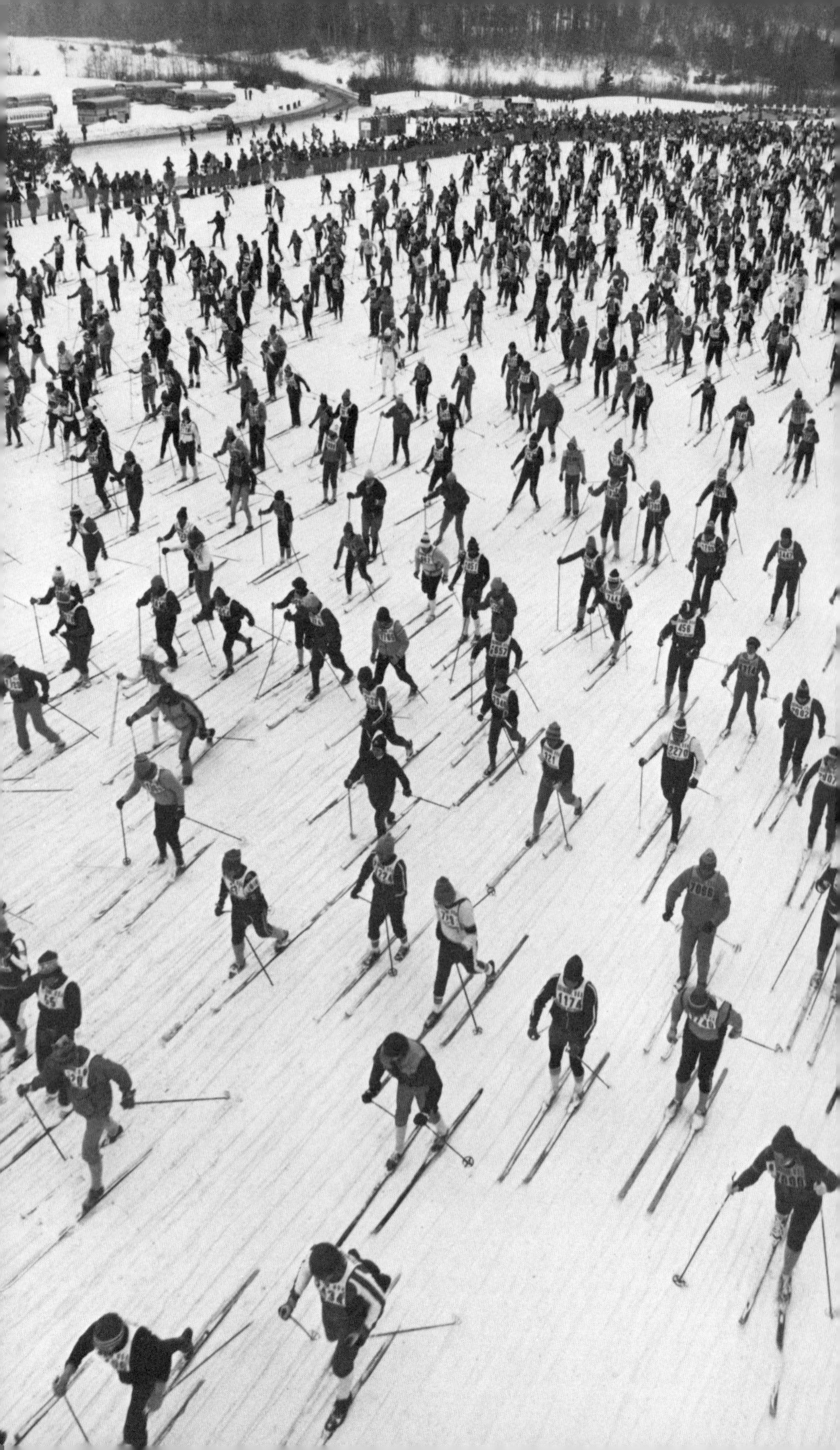

CONTENTS

   Preface 9
   Acknowledgments 11
1 What Lies Ahead 13
2 Training 35
3 Roller Skiing 55
4 The Inner Racer 61
5 Technique 73
6 Waxing 111
7 Equipment and Clothing 137
   Race Organization 171
   Ski Associations and Races 173
   Recommended Reading 174
   Glossary 177
   Index 185

The start of the American Birkebeiner, Wisconsin. (Tom Kelly photo)

PREFACE

Although we were living on different continents when we met each other in the early 1960s, we were both involved in writing about cross-country skiing. So we half jokingly formed the AABCCE, which stands for American Association of Books on Cross-Country in English. The best part of this two-person organization has been the exchange of information about what's happening in cross-country skiing in Europe and America. It was probably only natural that we would eventually write a book together.

In looking over the literature, we realized there was no book available that would help and encourage the citizen racer—the cross-country skier who has learned the basics and would like to improve his technique and endurance through fast, long-distance touring in the company of fellow skiers. So we decided to write one.

Entering a citizens' race is something like preparing for an extended backpacking trip in the mountains—planning is half the fun. Studying the

Auran ski club, Lemi, Finland, ca. 1910. The first known photo of women cross-country ski racers. (Aamulehti of Tampere photo)

terrain, organizing your equipment, getting ready psychologically, even taking some shorter training tours are all part of preparing for the big day.

Citizens' racing is sixty years old on the international scene. In North America it is far younger—the first major citizens' races were held in the early 1960s. During the last two decades the number of races, the variety of equipment and waxes, and enthusiasm for the sport have accelerated to a point where thousands are now enjoying it.

Like racing in the world of running, cross-country ski racing is divided into two major categories. Classified or sanctioned races correspond with track events in running. These are highly organized ski races—the stuff of Winter Olympic Games and World Ski Championships. Entry is restricted to athletes classified by national ski associations.

Citizens' races, on the other hand, correspond with the "fun runs," road races, and mass marathons of the jogging-running world. Also known as touring races, ski marathons, loppets, and a variety of other names, their focus is on the joy of participation. The designation "citizen," now the standard term throughout the skiing world, means that the races are open to everyone.

The appeal of citizens' racing is that it's just plain fun. Races are often miniature wilderness experiences, and no matter what your level of ability, there is always a challenge to meet. We still get as much of a kick out of entering a citizens' race today as we did when we thought we were going to burn up the tracks as teenagers. Not long ago we talked with a gentleman who had just finished the trans-mountain Birkebeiner race in Norway and found he had the same view. He was seventy-six years old.

As a citizen racer, you are free to set your own goals. You can be as carefree or serious as you wish. This book touches on both extremes, giving you the background for serious involvement and improvement, yet encouraging you to retain the joy that is citizens' racing. After all, enjoyment is the essence of the sport.

John Caldwell
Putney, Vermont
Michael Brady
Oslo, Norway

ACKNOWLEDGMENTS

To our wives, we owe gratitude for tolerating the haphazard lives that authors lead while striving to meet publishers' deadlines. To a friend and the photographer of this book, Fletcher Manley, we are indebted for an unusual understanding of the subject. Thanks also to Ole Mosesen, who set track after track after track so we could photograph technique studies. Photographer and avid citizen racer Frits Solvang contributed time and professional skills for many illustrations—both his own work and historical archive shots. And last but not least, thanks go to the crew at The Mountaineers Books—John Pollock, Donna DeShazo, and Ann Cleeland—for so meticulously following the publication through from start to finish.

Tour race start at Waterville Valley, N.H. (Joan Eaton photo)

1
WHAT LIES AHEAD

If you're a recreational cross-country skier and find ordinary touring a bit tame, it's time to consider citizens' racing. You don't need to be young or a jock to participate. The point of the sport is not necessarily to be the first over the finish line; for most of the thousands of skiers who enter ski touring races every year, the joy of racing is its *challenge*, or how it tests their capabilities. If they all worried about their performances relative to some of the real hotshots on the circuit, some of whom are former Olympians, they probably wouldn't enter in the first place. Most citizen racers have learned to set standards for themselves in training and in racing, and no matter what their standards are, they feel as much satisfaction in meeting them as the faster racers do in meeting theirs.

Like competitive running, distance ski racing requires considerable training and involvement, both physical and mental. Each race is the ultimate challenge of mind and body striving for an objective. This book is about the preparation and background that will get you to a race. The rest is up to you.

A FEW "RULES"

At the outset, we'll make a few observations that we think are nigh onto rules for the sport:

- **Avoid the complicated.** Unfortunately, citizens' racing has attracted some faddists. Among these are some latter-day, self-proclaimed gurus of the sport who make everything about it very special and very mystical. Listening to them, you might be led to believe that you cannot possibly ski well, let alone race, unless you become party to a whole new world of knowledge.

To that we reply with a single word: rubbish! Skiing is no strange activity, and racing is part of skiing. Almost everything that can be said about the subject has natural parallels in your daily experience off snow. For example, hit the brakes of your car a bit hard on a wet asphalt road, and you feel the effect of the same low friction that makes ski glide on snow possible. Carry a pail of paint up a stepladder, and you have a body position that isn't bad for ascending hills on skis. So that's why we explain things as we do in this book, likening ski racing techniques and so on to daily experiences in order to eradicate strangeness and make it familiar.

- **Pay attention to the factors that will most affect race performance.** The most important factors are your overall physical condition, skiing ability, wax, equipment, and clothing, in that order, with a big gap in importance between the first three and the last two.

- **Resist the temptation to focus on details.** Many racers make the mistake of perfecting minutia while letting gross problems go by. Remember, a

perfectionist usually isn't in love with the sport; he is in love with some ideal.
- **Don't worry about worrying.** Pre-race jitters are probably more common than you think. The cool heads at the starting line are usually the people with experience, so they hide their emotions better than other racers. Besides, a bit of self-generated excitement often helps. If you can't get fired up about racing, why do it?
- **Beware of gimmicks and gadgets.** They come and go; it would take a book thicker than this one just to list and describe all the off-the-wall inventions that have been pushed in the last ten years alone. If anyone has a short-cut method or item to offer, find out what's in it for him before you bite.
- **Enjoy yourself.** Need we say more?

THE CALL IS WORLDWIDE

Citizens' racing started in Scandinavia, so the conduct of the sport and many of the names associated with it have Nordic roots. The suffix -*loppet* in

---

What's in a Name?

Cross-country skiing is a long name for a simple sport.

Once there was only one type of *skiing*, a utilitarian form of over-snow winter transport. The young daredevils made sport of it and leapt through the air on skis. *Ski jumping* was born.

In 1932 when the third Winter Olympic Games were held in Lake Placid, the competitive form of skiing was called *long-distance ski racing*. About that time, a new group of ski addicts devised downhill-only competitions, and in 1931 the *downhill ski runners* held their first international races in Mürren, Switzerland. Their events came first on the 1936 Olympic calendar.

Ski competition was blotted out for a decade by World War II. When it reappeared, the newer events had been renamed *alpine skiing*.

The first time that postwar North America saw international competition on home snow was the 1950 World Ski Championships, and then again in the 1960 Winter Olympics at Squaw Valley and the 1980 Winter Olympics at Lake Placid. Meanwhile, it was *alpine skiing* that had captured the fancy of recreational skiers, and somehow *alpine* got dropped. That form of the sport became *skiing*.

So what was the original form of skiing to be called when it blossomed into a full-scale renaissance in the early 1970s? Borrowing from the sport of track and field, the term *cross-country skiing* was chosen.

Thus, an old sport was given a new name—and a long one, at that. But in cross-country skiing circles, everyone knows what you're up to when you say you're going skiing—cross-country, of course!

a race name, for instance, comes from the Vasaloppet, the Swedish granddaddy of them all. The word Birkebeiner in a name, such as the American Birkebeiner or the Australian Birkebeiner, comes from the trans-mountain citizens' race by that name in Norway. Much of the sport's lore lies in these two races, so we'll say something about each of them, and then give you a sampling of their cousins in other countries.

Throughout this discussion we'll give you the best times recorded at this writing, when those times are available. Even though snow conditions and course profiles play a large part in skiing times, and even though we are not trying to set records ourselves, these times do give us a good indication of the time it would take us to ski the courses. All we have to do is add 40 percent—or is it 50 or 60 percent?

Vasaloppet

Every country has its major historical figure, and for the Swedes it's Gustav Vasa. A leader in the uprising against Danish King Kristian II, Vasa was a wanted man, and in the winter of 1520-21 he fled for his life toward Norway. At Sälen, he was overtaken by two loyal scouts who persuaded him to return, lead the rebellion, and become king of Sweden.

In 1921, during the quadricentennial celebration of Vasa's emancipation of his country, a commemorative race was planned. At 6:00 A.M. on March 19, 1922, 119 men started at Sälen to ski the 85.6-km course of Vasa's return journey to Mora. It was the first Vasa race, or Vasaloppet, in Sweden.

The Vasaloppet is listed in the *Guinness Book of World Records* as the world's largest ski race. The number of racers has increased steadily through the years, peaking at 12,000 in 1980. The first Vasaloppet was won in just over seven and one-half hours, while the record time over the fixed course to date is Ola Hassis's 1979 win in 4.5.49 (4 hours, 5 minutes, and 49 seconds).

The Blueberry Book of Records

The world's oldest and largest ski race, the Vasaloppet, annually attracts about 9,000 Swedes and about 1,500 foreigners from as many as twenty other countries. Organizing and running the race takes a staff of 2,000. Transporting the racers' gear from the start to the finish takes thirty large trucks. Spectators line the course at all access points and where the tracks go through villages and towns; for an average race, they number 35,000.

At the six feeding stations, the racers consume over 13,000 gallons of warm Swedish *Blåbär* (blueberry) drink, and the after-race dinner in Mora dishes out three and one-half tons of potatoes, two tons of meat, two tons of vegetables, and nine tons of table drink. The food is badly needed. In completing the 85-km course, the average racer loses four to five pounds, mostly through liquid depletion. That's equivalent to having 280 racers disappear completely during the course of the event.

In 1981 the race was officially opened to women, and the first female winner was Meeri Bodelid with a time of 5.28.08.

Race date: First Sunday in March

Address: Vasaloppet, Vasagatan 17, 79200 Mora, Sweden

Birkebeiner

Like the Vasaloppet, the Birkebeiner race, or Birkebeiner-rennet in Norwegian, commemorates a historical incident involving a winter journey taken by a king-to-be.

As civil war raged, the infant heir to the throne, Haakon Haakonssoen, was sought by the warring Clericals. So, in January, 1206, two loyalist scouts

In Vasaloppet the long-distance skier has company. (Studio 9 photo)

strapped on their skis and fled with the baby, carrying him over a mountain plateau to safety in another valley. There, a peasant loaned them horses, and they took the infant north to Nidaros (now Trondheim), where he grew up to become the king who ended the civil wars and first forged a united Norway. The loyalist scouts were called "Birch Legs," or Birkebeiner in Norwegian, after the custom of wrapping their legs up to their knees with birch bark for protection as they skied through deep mountain snow.

The course of the race commemorating the feat of the Birkebeiner scouts stretches 55 km from Lillehammer to Rena, Norway, and crosses an intervening mountain plateau. It's run in different directions in alternate years; the direction from Rena to Lillehammer is regarded as the tougher, as the total vertical climb from Rena to the height of the plateau is a whopping 750 m (2,500 ft). Racers must carry a pack weighing at least 5.5 kg (a little over 12 lb), the symbolic weight of the infant carried by the scouts.

The first Birkebeiner-rennet was held in 1932 and was won in just nine minutes under five hours. The race has been held every year since, with the exception of the war years 1941-45. The best times to date are held by Dag Atle Björkheim: 3.02.43 in 1982 for the Rena-Lillehammer direction, and 3.05.39 in 1977 for the Lillehammer-Rena direction. Anna Bjoergan has the

---

Reverse, Anyone?

Cross-country race courses are described in numbers: length, height difference between lowest and highest points, maximum climb, and total climbs in traversing the course. But courses with identical numerical measurements can offer different challenges, and even the challenge of a single course can vary, depending on the direction in which it is run.

The courses around Lahti, Finland, where the 1978 World Ski Championships were held, are a good example. The uphills are long and gradual; if you ski them flat out, you sprint the course. The downhills are short and steep, so fast that racers have little time to rest. At Lahti, the racers and coaches agreed; it seemed that you worked all the time.

There was a dissenting voice, an American ski reporter. He skied some of the course loops one day by himself and found he had no difficulties on the downhills. So he wrote that the courses were "easy."

His colleagues wondered why he had misjudged the courses. Perhaps he didn't understand the sport well enough to know that racers use downhills for resting. But he had skied the courses the wrong way, herringboning up a few short, steep hills, to coast gloriously on the downhills. For him, the courses allowed lots of resting.

Direction dictates difficulty. Think of that whenever you assess a course.

The Norwegian Birkebeiner race winds through farming country before climbing up to a mountain plateau. (J. Klassen photo)

women's Rena-Lillehammer record of 3.47.15 set in 1980, and Valborg Oestberg the Lillehammer-Rena record of 3.31.04 set in 1977.

Race date: Third or fourth Sunday in March

Address: Birkebeiner-rennet, Rena Idrettslag, 2450 Rena, Norway

A Round-the-World Roundup

The overall idea of all citizens' races is the same, but each has a distinct character. Sample a few citizens' races, and you'll see what we mean. Join us on a worldwide tour of the World Loppet, the league of major races in eight different countries besides Sweden and Norway. The World Loppet is an American idea and includes the undisputed greats, the Vasaloppet and the Birkebeiner. The secretariat for the World Loppet is at the Telemark Lodge,

Cable, Wisconsin 54821; you can write there for information on entries to all World Loppet races, and on World Loppet Tours to the races abroad. There's even a World Loppet Passport, which offers several advantages, including a mound of detailed information on the races.

Finland–Finlandia Hiihto

Even the most casual observer of the cross-country ski scene knows that if there is one thing at which the Finns excel, it's cross-country skiing in all its varieties. Finland is made for cross-country skiing, so it's no wonder that the biggest Finnish citizens' race, the Finlandia Hiihto, though barely a decade old, is now second only to the Vasaloppet in size. The race winds 75 km through forests and past frozen lakes, from Hämeenlinna to Lahti, where several World Ski Championships have been held. It's divided into classes, as are the other citizens' races, but also features a "Sunday Skier" class for those who want to race but not against the clock. Record time over the course is just under four hours and fifteen minutes, set by Matti Kuosku.

Race date: A Sunday in early March
Address: Finlandia Hiihto, Hämeenkatu 5, 15110 Lahti 11, Finland

Switzerland–Engadin Skimarathon

By far the most scenic experience in all of citizens' racing, the 42-km Engadin Skimarathon winds along a valley in the very heart of the Alps, passing St. Moritz and Pontresina and other living legends of mountaineering and alpine skiing. The course is fairly flat, and, in the good tradition of

The dawn line-up for a major race start can be awesome; this is the Finlandia Hiihto. (Studio LK photo)

Swiss hospitality, is lined with racer services. The fastest skier of the course finished in less than foot-marathon time; he is American Bill Koch, whose 1981 time was 2.00.18.

Race date: A Sunday in mid-March
Address: Engadin Skimarathon, CH-7514 Sils/Segl, Switzerland

Austria –Dolomitenlauf

Winding 60 km through mountainous scenery in the East Tirol of Austria, this race vies with the Engadin in Switzerland for the best views.

Race date: A Sunday in mid-January
Address: Post Box 1000, A-9900 Lienz, Austria

Germany –König Ludwig Lauf

Germany is the country where the slogan for cross-country skiing is "Langläufer Leben Länger" ("Cross-country skiers live longer"). Here the spectrum of citizens' races boggles the mind. The country's major international event, the König Ludwig Lauf, is a stratified race, offering four race distances: 10 km, 20 km, 40 km, and 90 km. All tracks curve through the alpine valleys around Oberammergau. Racer services abound, local village mayors show up to wish the competitors well, and there are even events for kids. Pauli Siitonen set the 90-km record in 1976 when he skied the course in 3.59.38.

Race date: Saturday and Sunday, late January or early February
Address: König Ludwig Lauf, D-8103 Oberammergau, West Germany

France –Transjurassienne

The Vasaloppet winner gets a wreath around the neck as the symbol of achievement. But in eastern France and northwestern Switzerland, in the Jura Mountains where the dairy industry is strong, the symbol for the leading human in a race is the same as for the leading cow of a herd: a huge cowbell. The course winds 76 km through farm towns, from Lamoura to Mouthe, and annually attracts over 2,000 racers. Records on the course are 3.29.51 for men by Sven-Åke Lundbäck in 1981, and 4.20.16 for women by Marie Christine Subot in 1981.

Race date: A Sunday in mid-February
Address: Transjurassienne, Progressieme du Jura,
   Hôtel de Ville, 39400 Morez, France

Italy –Marcialonga

At 70 km, the Marcialonga isn't the longest citizens' race but is considered the most entertaining. Running along the Avisio River Valley from Canazei to Cavalese, it passes through dozens of mountain villages, with names sounding as if they had been lifted from an opera libretto. The start is at Moena, about 18 km south of Canazei. The course heads north to Canazei, then doubles back past Moena, goes through Predazzo, and finishes at Cavalese. In each town and village, the locals turn out in force to watch the racers ski down their main streets. The air is alive with a vitality that only the Italians seem capable of providing; each race provides new stories of just

(Top)*Racing is for kids, too; 1.2-km mini-citizens' race, Childrens' Championship Day, 1982, Oslo, Norway. (Michael Brady photo)*
(Bottom) *The home stretch of the Holmenkollmarsjen race in Oslo, Norway. (Michael Brady photo)*

how much fun it is to be cheered along in Italian and half-a-dozen other languages, no matter what your position in the race.

The Marcialonga is about half the size of the Vasaloppet: its record number of racers was 6,880 (of which 6,003 finished) in 1974. The speediest racers set their records in 1981: Sven-Åke Lundbäck at 3.19.36 for men, and Canins Maria Bonaldi at 3.56.13 for women.

Race date: Usually a Sunday in late January

Address: Marcialonga Secretariat, I-38037 Predazzo (Trento), Italy

Canada – Rivière Rouge Race

In lake-studded country between Montreal and Ottawa, the Rivière Rouge follows a 55-km looped course around Lachute, Quebec. There are no individual climbs of more than about 90 m (300 ft), and winning times are fast, usually less than three hours.

Race date: A Sunday in early February

Address: Rivière Rouge Race, P.O. Box 69, Ottawa, Ontario K1N 8V3, Canada

The start of the American Birkebeiner covers an alpine ski slope with cross-country racers. (Tom Kelly photo)

U.S.A.–The American Birkebeiner

The American Birkebeiner isn't just the largest ski race in North America and the fourth largest in the world; it's also the race that offers the optimum blend of European tradition and the American way of doing things. It has an exchange agreement with the original Birkebeiner in Norway: the fastest U.S. man and woman in the American Birkebeiner get a free trip to compete in the Birkebeiner in Norway, and vice versa. There is even a race newspaper called the *Birch Scroll*, and events surround the competition for a week in late February. The race starts at Hayward, Wisconsin, and winds 55 km through the northwoods country to the finish at the Telemark Lodge at Cable, Wisconsin. There's also a half-distance event called the Korteloppet (a blend of Norwegian and Swedish words for "short race").

Fifty-eight racers showed up at the start of the first American Birkebeiner in 1973, and by 1981 the total number had swelled to 7,000. The trails put in by the Telemark Lodge, including the American Birkebeiner Trail, are probably the most carefully manicured on the continent. The men's record time for the old 55-km course from Cable to Hayward is 2.24.55, set in 1980 by Per Knotten, while the fastest women's record is held by Gry Oftedal, with a time of 2.53.48 in 1980. In mentioning speed in the race, we can't resist the temptation to brag just a bit: John Caldwell's daughter Jennifer, despite breaking her hand at the 17-km point, was the fastest U.S. woman in 1980, with a time of 2.56.01; Michael Brady's wife, Marianne Hadler, was overall women's winner of the 1981 race.

If you get into citizens' racing seriously, sooner or later you'll probably make that trip from Cable to Hayward.

Race date: Usually a Sunday in late February
Address: American Birkebeiner, Telemark Lodge,
  Cable, Wisconsin 54821

ENTERING A RACE

It's not difficult to enter a race. You simply find out about the event from a friend or in a ski association schedule or ski magazine, and then send in your entry blank and fee. It's the preparation that follows this action that's tough.

There are definite advantages to entering a long race months ahead of race day. It establishes a commitment on your part, so you are apt to spend more time in preparation. Being committed also means you're more likely to get a copy of the course profile and plan your training accordingly (see chapter 2). Also, the entry fee often is lower if you are early, and some races cut off entries after a certain number have been received.

If you have a choice between races in January or in March, choose the later one. You can be better prepared in March and the race might serve as a fitting climax to your season. Weather in January is usually colder and the days are shorter. These factors can cause a difference in daily training, racing, and recovery periods. Most knowledgeable coaching staffs do not schedule their national 50-km championships early in the season for fear that their elite skiers might not recover for the remainder of the season when

A sport for kings: King Carl Gustaf of Sweden racing the 1967 Vasaloppet. (Pressens Bild photo)

important international races are held. Even though your level of exertion does not necessarily match that of the elite skier, you can still be affected by the same problems.

TRAVEL

If you fly east-west and cross several time zones in traveling to a race, then you'll soon discover that jet lag affects your performance. This is because many human physiological functions, such as heart rate and body temperature, have distinct, rhythmic changes in the course of a twenty-four-hour day. These rhythmic changes are called *circadian rhythms*, and are apparently timed by several different biological clocks.

When the rhythms are upset, many things can happen. Exhaustion, slowed reactions, insomnia, and loss of appetite are some of the penalties paid for the luxury of the speed of jet aircraft travel. As racing requires your best performance, having one or two of your biological clocks off schedule will lessen your abilities.

What can you do about this if you must fly to a race? The answer depends on your goal in that race. Snapping out of jet lag takes time: the digestive system can accommodate at a speed of about one day for each hour of time difference involved. Heart rate doesn't return to normal until four to six days after flying long distances. You'll hardly notice a change of one hour; flying to a race in the next time zone isn't a problem. It's when you jump over four time zones or more that the difficulties arise. Racers experienced in trans-Atlantic travel have two remedies that seem to work fairly well.

First, try to get to the race time zone several days early. In other words, if you fly to a race in Europe, make it part of your annual vacation, and spend the first week overseas seeing sights and skiing for fun. Be careful the first two days, as for you it's rhythmically the middle of the night, the time when your circadian rhythms dictate low activity levels. After you've become a bit adjusted—on the third day or so—you can ski a bit more seriously, and after the fourth day you can go all out. This approach has disadvantages if you arrive at the race site several days early. Practice time sometimes is limited, because the organizers don't worry about final track preparation until just before the race. In addition, the added excitement of the race unfolding can be a bit wearing.

Another trick is to try gradual adjustment before you leave home. If you're flying to Europe, for instance, try adjusting for a week before you leave: push ahead by half-an-hour the time you get up, eat each meal, and go to bed. There are practical limitations to this plan, especially if you have a job or school work to take care of, or eat your meals with others. Most racers have found that two hours of preadjustment is about the limit they can handle. Using this approach, however, allows you to arrive at the course the day before the race, run the race, then take advantage of the skiing and lack of pressure afterward, really whooping it up for the rest of your vacation.

If you are close enough to drive to a race, you may want to travel to and from the race in a car pool with other skiers. The only problem you might have is if the driver is one of those casual people who is always late. You would be out of luck if you planned on pre-race time for changing clothes, waxing, and warming up, and you got to the race site only a few minutes before starting time. So, be sure your driver is the punctual type.

GEAR

It may sound like a ridiculous reminder to plan and pack well in advance so you don't leave any critical item behind. But we've known even experienced racers who have arrived at races minus the most unbelievable things: clothing, boots, poles, and yes, even skis. Besides your usual ski gear, clothing, and travel items, be sure to have the following:

- **A good ski bag.** Avoid road travel with skis exposed, such as on an auto roof-rack. Road film and road salt are two of the best-known oxidizers and etchers of ski materials. Bagged skis don't get dirty.

- **A convenient bag for your clothes.** A duffel bag is nice because it conforms to almost any shape required in a car trunk. Backpacks are a terror for car travel, and even airlines generally accept them as baggage only when they are wrapped in a tough plastic bag or packed in a protective box (in order to protect other baggage).

- **A small wax kit.** This is unbeatable for convenience when you have to wax at a race. The larger variety, the size of an obese attaché case, holds far more than you'll ever need at one race, but it is fine if there are several of you sharing the contents.

RACE DAY

Here it is. You know how well prepared all your training has made you. Don't overextend. Don't try second-guessing. Don't break up a winning combination during the pressure of race day. If, for example, a friend rushes up to you and suggests a wax you have never tried, leave it alone.

If you are well prepared, you will arrive an hour or so ahead of the starting gun and pick up your bib, start order, and start time. You then should have time to learn all you need to know about toilet locations, food stations, wax

Starts can be as simple as one pair at a time. (Michael Brady photo)

huts, the place for warm-ups and changes of clothing, shower facilities, transportation arrangements, flagging for the course, weather forecasts, temperatures, and recommended wax selection. You then can wax your skis and test them.

If you're assigned to start with one wave of skiers representing a certain age class, then that's what you do. But if the race is a mass-start affair with everyone starting together, place yourself according to the organizers' instructions or your expectations. Don't try to start in the front row if you don't expect to be skiing with the front-runners. Well-organized mass-start races have starting areas marked for skiers who expect to take five hours on the course, six hours, and so on. Start where you belong and you will help to avoid delays, pileups, broken equipment, unnecessary passing situations, and so on.

It's even a good idea to be conservative when estimating your finish time. In any 40-km or longer tour race, there is plenty of time to pass other skiers. A start with a slower group might be an important factor in your pacing. We have seen competitors get carried away with a fast start in fast company, only to collapse around the 20-km mark. They end up with slower times than usual.

During the race, the following tips might be helpful:

Keep your poles in close and don't try any skating steps during the start. You might get entangled.

If you can ski with a friend or group of friends, take turns with the lead. This allows others the drafting advantage—there's less wind resistance when you follow someone closely. Besides, you gain psychologically from good conversation.

Use a gimmick, such as a wager with a friend, for inspiration during the race. We do this ourselves and, as we know some good skiers, our bets go like this: If we finish within 35 percent of their time, we win the bet—usually some liquid refreshment. We have no illusions of grandeur but know, based on past performances, that such a wager is reasonable. Plus, we can set our standards according to their more consistent performances.

Bike Tactics

The advantage of drafting in biking is well known, and riders with less than top long-distance capabilities can keep themselves in contention by closely following teammates who take the lead for them, and break down wind resistance. What is not so well known is that drafting is also an advantage for skiers, though much less so than for bikers. As more skiers acquire more skill and more stamina, it will be the little things that separate them in the results. If one team of racers, for instance, has some good, strong skiers who can break track for their sprint man until the end of the course, we may have the same phenomenon we presently see in bicycle racing. Can you believe it?

In Finland it's cold, and warming stops are provided in the Finlandia Hiihto race. (Studio LK photo)

In general, play to your strengths. Don't bull it on an uphill if you really aren't strong in that area. Slow down and take it easy. Conversely, if you have a good double-pole, don't hesitate to use it.

Use all the food stations. Passing them by isn't good for your health.

Be alert to the trail conditions in case you come around for another lap.

Be aware of the kilometer markers so you can keep track of your pacing. Don't get overconfident and overextend yourself if you are ahead of pace. If you are behind pace, try to figure out why. Is the snow slow? Has most of the course been uphill, temporarily causing the slower pace? If your pace is off just because you are going too slowly, then step it up.

Conserve energy whenever possible. If you are skiing a lap course, you can always speed up near the end of the last lap. Remember, it's better to finish feeling good and wanting to do it again than to crawl across the line and collapse.

A "TYPICAL" RACE

No race is organized perfectly, but for those who have never skied in a citizens' race, it might help if we describe an ideal big tour race with a few thousand entrants. (A small race is basically the same—just smaller, less crowded, and less complicated.) Here's the way it "happened" for us.

After checking in at the course and familiarizing ourselves with everything we needed to know, we waxed our skis, then sat in the car and relaxed for about half-an-hour. With about ten minutes to go, we tagged our packs and put them in the allotted area near the start, where they would be picked up by the organizers and delivered to the race finish. Since the wax on our skis was holding, we began skiing around in the massive start area. Then we lined up and, just before the start, shed our warm-ups—complete with numbered tags—throwing them back over our heads to other skiers who threw them back farther. Finally they ended up in a pile where the organizers could sort and gather them, then take them to the finish.

It was a wave start, by age groups, and so there were only a few hundred skiers vying for the lead after the gun sounded. However, we knew that the next group would be starting in fifteen minutes and if we dawdled we would be overtaken by another wave of skiers. So we pushed along fairly hard until the trail narrowed to three lanes. We had been told that the right

Women now race the trans-mountain Birkebeiner race in Norway carrying the same 5.5-kg load required of men racers. (Swix photo)

lane was sacred—if you skied there no one would bother you with a cry of "Track!" The middle lane was for faster skiers, or those who wanted to pass someone in the right lane. The left lane was the express lane; we knew we should stay out of it unless we were really cruising.

Before we knew it we had gone past the 5-km mark. There was still plenty of company, as there would be during the whole race. We began to pass a few skiers wearing different colored bibs and knew they were the slower skiers from the group that had started ahead of us. That's okay, we thought. They're having fun.

We skied into the first food station area and, on both sides of the track, saw several long tables full of plenty of drinks available for the taking. We found an open slot, skied in and out quickly with our cup, and started the gentle downhill as we drank the liquid. We tossed the cup at one of the waste barrels (and missed) and started in again at race pace.

The initial excitement was over and we knew we had to settle down to business and get in a groove. There was still a long way to go. It was another 12 km to the next food station. This was a key section of the course, one

Feeding station in the Yukon Jack race, 1981. (Michael Brady photo)

where it would be important to set a reasonable pace. The tracks were near perfect and for a time we felt isolated—although we certainly weren't—in the woods, far from anywhere.

We began to get warm and took off our gloves, stuffing them in the top of our running suits. Soon we did the same thing with our hats. We knew, though, that we would need this clothing when we reached the long 3-km downhill. We passed a first aid station and barely took note of it. We had a good rhythm going.

Suddenly our trance was broken as we arrived at the second food station. This was one where we had planned to tank up, so we stopped and had one cup of food, grabbed a second one, and skied off. As we finished that cup, a skier from the wave behind us passed. Feeling good, we jumped in behind him and held on for several kilometers—until we got to a rather long, gentle climb. Then we started to go under, a feeling of numbness creeping up through our legs, and we knew we had to slow down. It was over to the right track for us, and a slow walk. We had blown it, at least for the time being. After 1 or 2 km we began catching more skiers in the right track and so we moved to the middle track. Our skis were fast and on the next downhill we ventured over to the express lane, only to be tracked by a wave of skiers that had started two intervals after us! Well, we weren't going so fast after all. Back to the middle track. Better stay there because it was getting crowded in the fast lane.

The next food station seemed like a haven, with skiers from five different waves moving in and out of the area. It was a bit like a busy intersection in a city—orderly but crowded. This was the last food station and we thought we could sprint for the finish, several kilometers away, but the sprint wasn't there. Now it was a question of finishing and we knew we had to maintain our pace.

Soon the whole tour became more enjoyable. We knew we would make it and would feel great, standing there in the shower, talking about the race with the other competitors. Our daydreaming continued for a long time until we were brought out of it seeing the finish a few hundred meters away. Some skiers were really sprinting now, but we were content to cruise in. We wondered how the timers would sort us all out, but the answer was forthcoming when we rounded the last corner. A couple of stewards were there directing us to various color-keyed finish chutes, obviously matching up with the color of our bibs.

When we got to the chute there was only one skier there, in the process of getting his award and time. We had made it—for our medal! In other words, we had finished within the prescribed time, which is calculated on the average time of the first five finishers in our class. The official handed us our medal, we skied on through, and there were all the packs and warm-ups, lined up by bib number. We found ours, picked them up, and headed for the showers. From then on, and for the next two or three days, it was just a series of reminiscences. The shower removed any sore spots we felt and we took a long time to dress—it felt so good to do it that way.

Then it was off to the dining room. Huge bowls of soup and stew were available. Tables were covered with baskets of bread and fruit, and once we

After 85.6 km in less than 4½ hours, the joy of winning shows; Sven-Åke Lundbäck winning the 1981 Vasaloppet. (Lars-Erik Klockner photo)

got our dishes in the line and gave up our food tickets, we could keep going back for more. The atmosphere was electric and as some of the older competitors came into the room and were recognized, cheers went up from their friends. Just before we left, a very official looking fellow came in and asked for our attention. He then awarded a silver plate to a competitor who had just finished his twenty-fifth race! The whole crowd stood up to applaud the old-timer. This signaled the end of the meal for many, and we followed them to the buses waiting to take us back to the start. When we drove away, a few of the skiers in the bus were still talking about the race, but now it was in muted tones. Most of us slept during the return trip.

RECOVERY AFTER A RACE

A natural tendency right after a race is to load up with liquids and food. Don't succumb to this desire. If you have been taking plenty of liquids on the course, you should not need a quart or two right after the race. Your body needs rest. Digesting a lot of liquid or solid food takes energy, and your stomach may not feel very well anyway. So take it easy.

A shower is a must if it is available. (Many race organizers simply do not have the facilities.) An alternative is to rub yourself with snow. This is invigorating and seems to help muscles recover faster than doing nothing at all. In any case, be sure to change your clothing and get into something warm and dry.

Studies have shown that people are most susceptible to colds right after a race, so doctors and coaches of top endurance skiers take these athletes out of circulation as much as possible. You may have other ideas and want to join the post-race celebrations. This is the dealer's choice. After all, few sports offer such after-event pleasures. Besides, you're relaxed. You feel high after completing the race and want to talk about it, with anyone. Congratulating others who finish the course helps create a kind of friendship to be remembered for a long time.

On the days following the event, there is no reason to avoid skiing if you have trained well and paced yourself during the race. In fact, you may still be on a high and will want to get out and cruise. Hard workouts are not advisable, however. Take it easy on the uphills, but don't waste a day thinking you must take no exercise. Your body will give you the best signals; listen to it.

34

2
TRAINING

If there is another area of skiing where people are continually looking over their shoulders more than they do with training, we are not acquainted with it. Thousands of competitive skiers, it seems, come up with something once or twice a year in the hope that each new regimen will bring them to the top. The fact is that some of the most isolated athletes have the best training programs because they believe in them, follow them consistently enough to be able to measure progress, and have the peace of mind that comes with fewer complications (resulting, in part, from not trying out new training tactics).

The most important aspect of any training program for any endurance sport is to establish a long-term commitment to a lifestyle that includes endurance training. It's as simple as that! If you can mesh endurance training with your job, family, and surroundings, and if the training enhances your life, you've got it. This commitment to a lifestyle is far more important than any specialized, scientifically designed program that incorporates specificity training, intervals, speed work, fartslek, strength work, anaerobic threshold exercises, development of fast or slow twitch fibers, altitude training, or anything else fresh from various sources. Even some of our Olympians would probably be better off if they took a more basic approach to training.

TRUTHS OF TRAINING

Don't interpret our introductory remarks to mean that we're soft on training. We know that all other things being equal, the best-trained skier usually wins. And we personally know hundreds of examples, from top international classified racing to strictly local fun meets, where training background is primary. Without it, you're nowhere in racing. So we preface our remarks on the subject with a few observations that we regard as the truths of training:

1. Lots of racing requires lots of training. You simply cannot be a dedicated ski racer in the winter without having been a dedicated off-snow trainer the rest of the year. Somewhere there's a factor that relates duration of training to duration of competition. Top experts can't pin it down, but the trend is obvious. Think of track and field events, for instance. Marathon runners obviously put in more time training than do, say, pole vaulters. If you aim to ski several endurance races per season, your hopes will be

(Top, left) *A roller board provides exercise that is specific to cross-country racing. It can be easily constructed — the movable sled in the center of the board is mounted on chair casters. (John Caldwell photo)*

(Bottom) *A crucial part of any good outdoor gym is this "dip machine." (John Caldwell photo)*

dashed if you haven't put in several training stints of equivalent duration beforehand.

2. Skiing is about the best training there is. There is no hiding the fact that the best route to being a good ski racer is to do a lot of skiing. We've seen some comic cases of dedicated training faddists running on foot, roller skiing, or whatever when they had quite acceptable skiing close at hand. Top racers do try to run occasionally during the ski season just so their running muscles don't go stale and backfire on them in the transition from skiing to running in the spring. But you don't see them running often after the first snow falls.

3. Training isn't racing. Whatever you do, don't compete with others when you're out training. It's ruinous. Consider the all-too-typical situation of a gang of skiers training together. They go out for a distance workout. After awhile, one is in the lead and the rest are strung out behind. And so they go, sometimes changing positions, vying for the lead. The person ahead often is going just a wee too fast for his own good, and is running up a good-sized oxygen debt. The last person does the same thing, just trying to keep up. It's discouraging for everyone.

Don't compete in training. Leave your start-number bib at home.

4. Training is individual; there are no shortcuts. We can't say this enough. Often you hear that so-and-so did such-and-such last summer, and is skiing faster this year. Aha! He must have discovered the secret! If you find yourself falling for such a story, review all the facts. What else did the individual do? Give up smoking? Start eating less? Take a different job that requires more exercise? The parameters are endless.

We know that you would love to have a concise program, a direct guide to what to do. There are many such programs, and we have had a hand in devising some of them. But they are aimed at an integrated "team" of coach and racer who are working together. So we'll come right out and say it: No training program devised thus far will suit your needs exactly unless you have some help in interpreting, readjusting, and bending the guidelines as you go. So you won't find concise programs here. (There are some listed, however, in "Recommended Reading.")

5. Training efficiency depends on your lifestyle. You don't have to turn your life into a continual physical education class to do well at training. But you must be aware of influences on training. There are many; we list those we consider most important:

- Sleep. Get lots of it, regularly.

- Rest. After training, it's a must. The best recipe is a nap or serious loafing after training for the same length of time as you trained.

- No smoking. Let's face it—most training for cross-country ski racing aims at improving your ability to process oxygen, starting at your mouth and ending in your muscles. Your lungs have a big say in that process. Don't reduce their vote by smoking.

- Careful with alcohol. We're not puritans in this department, nor have we seen evidence that total abstinence leads to racing success.

6. Routine is vital. Frequent and easy is far superior to seldom and hard.

If you're serious about the sport, there's no such thing as "preseason training"; it's an ongoing affair that is part of your lifestyle. Among the Norwegians, who are perhaps better at the sport than most, there is a saying in training circles: "A day without training is a day without meaning" (it rhymes in Norwegian).

There are some basic principles that form a part of any successful training program. That's what the rest of this chapter is all about. We've written it primarily for the skier whose goal is to complete successfully one or two long tour races each year. The shorter races have their place in the scheme of things but do not involve such major preparations, either physical or mental. Much of the following material, however, will also be helpful to the skier who enters the shorter races.

DISCIPLINE

Your training season is a good time to get rid of all the excuses that invariably impede working out. Consider the following scenarios:

- The weather is inclement on a big training day. What do you do? Ask yourself what you will do in similar weather on race day. If you are deter-

Drill work is a fun method of practicing techniques and making small adjustments in them. Here the lead skier sets the pace and the whole crowd keeps the cadence with voice signals. (John Caldwell photo)

Ski-striding with or without poles is a good summertime exercise; you can even simulate the herringbone if you try. (John Caldwell photos)

mined to race in such conditions, then you had better get out there and practice.

- A friend shows up unexpectedly and wants to see you. This is tough, but if you let people know you are committed to training, they should not be upset if you are not available.

- You wake up with a scratchy throat on the day scheduled for a long workout. Ask yourself some questions. Would this throat prevent me from racing? What experiences do I have in training or racing under these conditions? Don't go out if you are truly ill, but don't be overly cautious either.

We prescribe a little determination in cases such as these.

MATCH WORKOUTS TO THE RACE

The most satisfying race results occur when race day is simply a repeat of your workouts. This practice, with the added excitement of race day, provides the atmosphere for your best performance.

So that you train on similar terrain as that of the race course, get a map or course profile of your race and study it. It's not very useful to train on short, choppy, steep ups and downs, for example, when your race has long climbs of 4 to 8 km.

Build up your training distances so you eventually ski the same length as the race course. If that distance is impractical for your conditioning or the area in which you're able to train, try to work out for the same amount of time you intend to be on the course. If you want to do 55 km in five hours, for example, make your last training sessions five hours long, even if you don't go the full 55 km.

It's a good idea to train during the time of day when the actual race will take place, usually in the morning. The advantage of this comes on race day, when one more item falls naturally into place.

Set a time to begin training. If you decide on 9:00 A.M. and don't get off the

---

Only if the Earth Moves

Training attitudes are often reflected in race results.

One summer, a friend named Mike Gallagher was staying with me in Oslo, Norway. That year there was only one rainless day from May through September. Gallagher trained twice a day. He had four sets of clothing and shoes that were continually in stages of drying out. One evening a dinner guest noted the array draped over all the radiators in the apartment and asked Gallagher if there were inclement conditions when he wouldn't train. "Sure is," Gallagher replied. "I'd be scared to death to go out and run if there was an earthquake on!"

Gallagher went on to be one of the best U.S. racers of his generation and is now the U.S. Ski Team National Cross-Country Ski Racing Coach. —MB

mark until 9:15, you had better figure out why you needed that extra fifteen minutes. A delay of fifteen minutes on race day might be crucial.

Your meal habits should also be compatible with the race schedule. This is described in the "Eating" section later in this chapter.

Your workouts should include at least one practice wax test. See what it would be like to train for the duration of your workout with the wax you select. In case it doesn't work, take along the items you'd need for rewaxing on the course.

PROGRESSIVE TRAINING

The body is a wonderful invention. For one thing, it's the most adaptable organism in existence. This is why progressive training works. You slowly up the dose of training, and the body becomes accustomed to that increased load and performs accordingly.

However, be careful about your progressions. If you are just launching on a program, you might have to begin by walking or biking easily, just a few miles a day. The increases can come in either the amount of time you exercise or in the intensity with which you exercise, or in both areas. Don't rush it. If you want to build up from a fairly inactive status, consider training for two or three years before expecting significantly improved results.

Teenagers who are eager to make the big time in skiing competition should increase their training load 10 to 20 percent every year and they might eventually reach the rather high distance figures of 1,000 km per month in their early twenties. But there will come a point, as with anyone else, when training can no longer be progressive in terms of distance or intensity.

Your training, too, might level off after a few years. It should decrease in intensity as you get older. Don't feel you must continually progress. Use common sense.

STRENGTH AND SPECIFICITY TRAINING

Strength is a tough subject to talk about in discussing training, as it means different things to different people, so misinterpretations are frequent. So we'll be short about it.

Doing any movement many times, as in cross-country ski racing, requires strength. Agility is determined by how fast you can make minor adjustments in position, which in turn also depends on muscular strength. If you're not strong enough to perform a given movement efficiently, you usually mobilize supplementary muscular force from areas less well suited to the task at hand; the inefficient use of the wrong muscles just tires you more rapidly.

To prepare yourself for citizens' racing, you need to use *specificity training*—you must train with exercise that is specific to the sport. The type of strength needed for cross-country skiing is not the ability to lift, push, or pull heavy weights, for instance. Therefore, body-building is just about the most useless preparation imaginable for this sport. Excess muscle bulk just means more baggage for you to have to drag along.

Bicycling is good endurance training. Biking in a group offers the advantages of companionship and the challenge of staying with the pack. (John Caldwell photo)

Few sports, if any, exceed cross-country skiing in the sheer number of muscles that are put to use. Consequently, your training should involve exercise that uses the maximum number of muscles. Roller skiing (see chapter 3), hiking or running with ski poles, and rowing offer the best training for cross-country skiing. This is not only because they involve so many muscles, but also because they require great *endurance*, a quality that is as important as strength in citizens' racing. Forget any of the stories you may know about the long-distance runner (and hence, in skiing terms, the long-distance skier) who collapses gloriously at the finish line. Get to the finish line completely exhausted and you're ensured of a place toward the tail of the result list. In other words, your strength must last.

If roller skiing, running, or rowing are not convenient for you, find some other form of endurance training that pleases you more, and engage in it wholeheartedly and regularly. Biking, kayaking, and canoeing are good alternatives. Your commitment to any form of exercise that significantly elevates your heart rate for an extended period of time is the overriding factor in a successful training program.

THE SENSIBLE APPROACH

Sports fans are often reminded that great athletes seem to be injury-free and healthy. If we all knew how these pros managed this we might become pros ourselves.

One thing is becoming increasingly clear. Injuries, and often sickness, follow a sudden change of activity. For instance, going from snow skiing to hard spring running is asking for trouble. Or going from a fall running program into long-distance skiing can bring on all sorts of problems the first few days.

So, whenever you change your training routine and launch into a new phase, begin very slowly. And ease out of the old routine slowly, whenever possible.

Also, forget all those stories you may have heard about individuals who can "train themselves out of a cold." Fresh air is fine. But pushing up your pulse is hardly the way to get rid of most illnesses, including simple colds. Treat them with respect. If we could tell you how to avoid them altogether, we would surely follow the advice ourselves. We do try to avoid getting tired and we watch out for crowds, but who knows if this helps? However, there is some evidence that skiers are particularly susceptible to sickness right after a race. It would follow that the same conditions exist right after a tough workout. Keep this in mind.

If you train on three or more successive days, establish a routine of alternating a harder day with an easier day. Your body needs a day to recover after a hard workout, and taking an easier day also can whet your appetite for the next day's training.

No matter how hard or easy your workout is, you should find some enjoyment in it and want to do it again, the next day, or the day after. If during the workout you wonder what you're doing there or think you'll never go through it again, you're simply pushing too hard. Save it. There is always tomorrow, or next week, or next month, or next year.

Running through thigh-deep water is deceptively hard and a good exercise for skiing. (John Caldwell photo)

No program, however carefully planned, can anticipate every little problem. Sometimes your body—the final authority on training—sends a signal to slow down. When this happens, do slow down, whether it's for a moment, a day, or a week. When you lose your spunk, when your legs ache, when you can't seem to slide one ski ahead of the other, rest up! Don't always believe you're taking it easy on yourself just because you can't do what you had planned.

MAKING UP FOR LOST TIME

If you are injured and lose some training time, what do you do when you get back on your feet?

Again, take it easy. Don't even consider trying to make up for lost time. Depending on your problem, you may have to go very slowly for a significant amount of time, testing yourself as you go along. Use your workouts to build confidence.

The best thing you can do during the lost days is to imagine how nice it's going to be when you do get back to your regular exercise. We have laid in hospital beds after leg operations and dreamed about being able to run again, and we have been sick and have imagined what pleasure it was going to be to get back on the trails. Be optimistic! It helps.

QUALITY TRAINING

There is a continuing controversy among professional cross-country skiers regarding the taking on of other activities besides training and skiing. Some coaches and national organizations practically insist that their athletes do nothing that will seriously affect their status as an athlete. Broadly interpreted, this often means no schooling, no work (even part time), no real outside commitments, and so on.

Some athletes who follow this approach are successful and some are not. Others, whether from necessity or from the belief that outside activities are important, take on such things as college or jobs. Some of them are successful and some are not. Thus the controversy.

Few of you reading this book have a choice. You have occupations other than training and skiing. Not to worry. Set your own standards and try to meet them. Don't get put off by others who spend large amounts of time skiing and training. You can't consider them in the same league as yourself.

But we will go further. We join the above controversy on the side of taking on other activities aside from training and skiing. We have seen lots of full-time athletes go great guns for a year or two, then begin to get stale, or quit. They probably get bored, or tired of the routine. They have ample time on their hands and thus training time actually gets devalued. A day comes when conditions are not just right and the full-timer knows he can postpone the workout. It even comes to the point where getting ready for the workout, cooling off, stretching, and showering take more time than the workout itself—just in order to help fill the twenty-four hours of the day.

Meanwhile, the athlete who takes on schooling or work will occasionally feel pushed for time. But he knows he has a more well-rounded life, that he

This variable-resistance exercise device for the arms can be mounted almost anywhere. (John Caldwell photo)

is working for something besides glory on the ski trails, and that he has a good possibility of a career after his competitive days are over. His time is so precious that he must engage in quality training. A day comes when he gets just one hour free. Do you think he spends a long time getting dressed, talking to friends, or taking a long shower?

We also know some young working couples with young children who still compete, but not with the Olympics in mind. When one can stay with the baby, the other gets a bit of time to train and really goes at it. Then they switch roles. When they go out together they take turns with their strength work, carrying the baby. All this is quality training, and they are skiing at least as well as they did when they had more time to train.

The point is not to be discouraged if you have only a small amount of time to train. Take advantage of this situation and put quality into your training. Plan a balanced program, stick with it, and you'll be amazed at how well you can do compared with "the good old days" when time was not so valuable.

THE TRAINING LOG AND THE OCCASIONAL TEST

If you want to learn about your training, or want to be sure about your progress, keep a simple training log, even if you train only a few times a week. Most people keep track of their workouts in terms of time and kilometers covered. Some keep weight figures, pulse rates, hours of sleep, and other notes on body signs. It's an individual matter.

One of the most important figures to keep track of is the time you take for an occasional test "run," whether it be on foot, on a bicycle, on roller skis, or on something else that is fairly constant. Do it once every couple of weeks, marking down the time and keeping it for reference. That way you can know if you are progressing.

PACING OR MONITORING

The goal of practicing pacing is to be able to pace yourself in race situations, the theory being that a well-paced race is the best race.

For a track runner, pacing is fairly easy. He simply times his quarters, laps, or set distances on a flat track. For someone running over terrain in the countryside or biking on hilly roads, it's another matter. Most people use a combination of body signals and information to determine their pace. Here are a couple of approaches:

- **Train on a hilly course.** Either running or biking, go just fast enough so that your breathing does not get labored and so that you can talk with a companion. This means you slow down on the uphills, go faster on the flats, and go about the same speed on the downs as you did on the flats. (There is not much to be gained by running fast down hills. You risk injury and, at the same time, achieve few training benefits. On the other hand, in biking you can work hard on the downhills and get some decent training. But be careful. Don't risk an accident.) Time yourself on this hilly course and mark it in your log. Keep on training for a couple of months and come back to try the course again, under the same conditions. If your elapsed time is faster

Ski-striding. (Fletcher Manley photo)

and you feel you have paced yourself as before, you will know you are in better shape.

    This method is very basic and requires that you be honest with yourself. If you can really do this, you will be best able to practice pacing in a race situation. However, most athletes have trouble with this system because so much depends on how you feel. Unless you have had extensive practice doing it, your times and effort are apt to vary widely.

- **Go to the track and run those quarters at specified times.** Check your own feeling against the time every lap. Learn what it feels like to exercise easily, so that you can talk as you go. After that, speed up for a series of laps and time them. See how long you can do this and register that feeling. The idea is to learn from your body's signals. Your breathing, the pounding of your heart, and the feeling in your legs and other muscles will tell you how much longer and how much faster you can go.

Going Under

Sooner or later when you are exercising, you are going to push just a bit too hard and experience the sensation of going under, going into oxygen debt, hitting the wall, or whatever you want to call it. It's best if this happens to you during training because the recovery time is often so long that any decent race time would be ruined by it.

Going under is associated with anaerobic exercise (see chapter 4). If you persist anaerobically long enough, you will surely go under and act a bit like a corpse. While many trainers and physiologists are touting the values of anaerobic training, which does not necessarily involve going under, we don't think that those of you reading this book need to practice this over and over. It is important, however, to be able to recognize the beginnings of going under and then to slow down. Your legs might tingle, your chest might get tight, your breathing might become labored. Register these feelings so that next time they come along you know enough to slow down.

Pulse Rates

We have been looking for information on optimum pulse rates for exercise for many years and several physiologists have told us that it is just impossible to prescribe. However, almost everyone agrees that pulse rates and

Does It Hurt?

Many people talk about the "pain" of distance events, including cross-country ski racing. It's an accepted part of the jargon, so much so that *Sports Illustrated*'s six-page, color-photo report on the 1970 FIS World Ski Championships was entitled "Don't Cry Until It's All Over." It focused entirely on the "pain" of cross-country ski racing, reporting that each racer is "alone in his own world of agony," which ends only at the finish line, when "they surrender to waves of fiery pain." Some coaches speak of training in terms of "no pain, no gain."

The world's top racers never speak of pain. Norwegians and Swedes, currently doing very well in international classified and citizens' cross-country ski racing, don't even have a word or phrase for it in their languages. Upon hearing an American speak of it during the 1972 Olympics, a Russian team doctor courteously inquired if he would like to have his injury examined.

There are good reasons for this apparent lack of appreciation of the term at the top. *Pain* is not an automatic ingredient of training and racing. It is one of the body's warning signals that something is wrong. When something hurts, you should stop, just as you would stop to take a rock out of your shoe when running or hiking.

Strain, however, is part of competition. In cross-country ski racing, strain is involved in mobilizing the body's resources to put out a large amount of power over a long period of time. If a racer misjudges the strain level and runs too hard, he may overwork anaerobically. This results in excess lactic acid buildup, which is felt as extreme discomfort or even pain. But when that point is reached, the muscles stop working and the racer goes under, and perhaps drops out of the race. Barring traumatic injury, pain in cross-country ski racing is part of quitting, not racing.

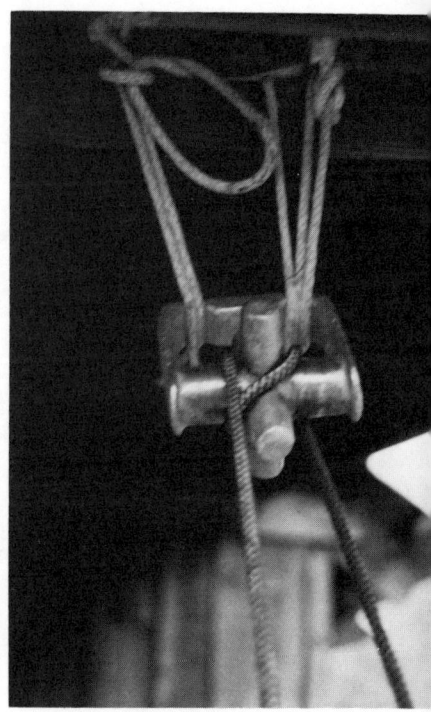

The device at right provides cord friction for arm exercise with ski pole straps. (John Caldwell photo)

oxygen uptake measurements are closely related. Therefore, the pulse rate is a fairly good indication of the amount of work one is doing during exercise.

A friend of ours, Brian Sharkey, published a chart of pulse rates for what he calls the aerobic training zone:

> Studies indicated the value of higher intensity training when it was increased *above* the aerobic threshold. The benefits were enhanced—to a point. When training became too intense, when the training heart rate was too high, the exercise became predominately anaerobic. Training beyond that point did not lead to additional improvements in aerobic fitness. Thus there seems to be an *aerobic training zone* that ranges from the training threshold (minimum training heart rate) to the anaerobic threshold (point of diminishing returns). Training at the lower end of the zone leads to predominately peripheral muscular training effects (if carried out for a sufficient duration). Training at the high end of the zone leads to central circulatory benefits.
>
> . . . For inactive individuals the training threshold is lower, as you would expect. If normal daily activity seldom exceeds a slow walk, a

brisk walk will elicit a training effect. Highly active and fit individuals have a higher training threshold. ... Thus the training zone for the fit will seem much too intense for the previously sedentary subject.*

AEROBIC FITNESS TRAINING ZONES

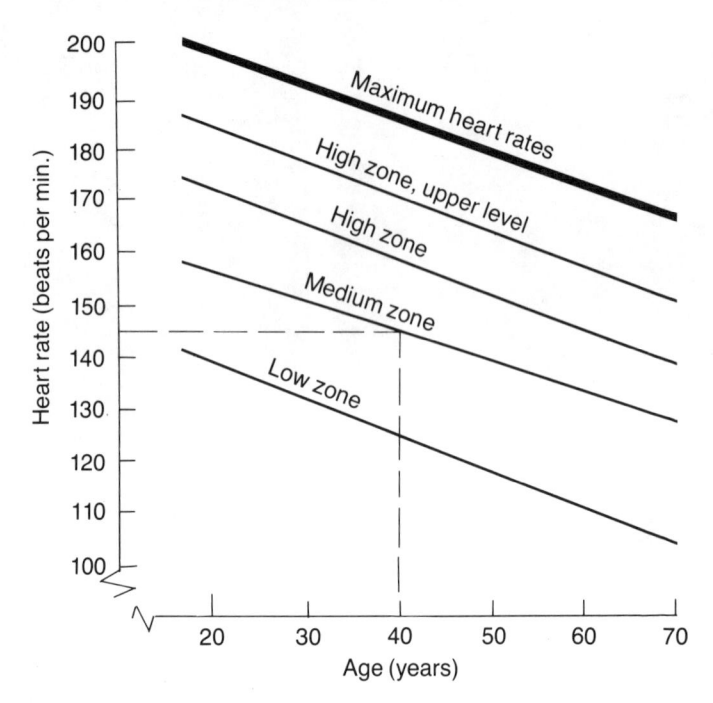

Aerobic fitness training zones. Use your age and fitness to locate your training zone. For 40 years of age and a low fitness score, zone = 125–142. (From Sharkey, 1979.)

To use the chart you must determine what level of fitness you are in. If you have been training regularly and lead a very active life, try the high fitness scale. If you are a few notches below this, use the medium level, and if you are just beginning, be conservative when you start and use the lower zone.

If you find that exercising at the upper level of the scale is too easy, reclassify yourself. Begin at the lower end of the next fitness scale. For instance, if you are forty and judge yourself to be in the lower-level fitness group, your optimum pulse rate for exercise would be in the range of 125 to 142 beats per minute. You should work in this interval. If you exercise with ease at 142 during your distance workouts, you should probably reclassify yourself as being in the medium fitness group. It's more likely that your

---

*Brian J. Sharkey, *Physiology of Fitness* (Champaign, Illinois: Human Kinetics Publishers, 1979), 39-40.

distance workouts would seem plenty tough for you at the 125 pulse rate level. Progressing up the scale would just be a matter of continuing to train to build yourself up.

The best way to check your pulse rate is to get a monitor that gives continual readings. Otherwise, you have to stop and take your pulse. However, after using the latter method often enough you might be able to make fairly accurate predictions without stopping to check your pulse.

You will be amazed at your heart rate when you go up hills. In order to stay within your recommended range you may find yourself walking the hills pushing your bike.

The Swedish Scale for Perceived Exertion*

The Swedes have come up with a system that has been sent to us by physiologist Ulf Bergh, who has written a book on the physiology of the sport (see "Recommended Reading"). It is less sophisticated and more conservative than Sharkey's aerobic training zone, but it has the same purpose—to help inexperienced people find a reasonable intensity for different types of training. The scale goes like this:

```
6
7   very, very easy
8
9   very easy
10
11  rather easy (as in distance training more than two hours)
12
13  somewhat strenuous (as in distance training under two hours)
14
15  strenuous (as in interval training)
16
17  very strenuous
18
19  very, very strenuous
20
```

From this you can see what the Swedes recommend for various workouts. The perceived exertion for distance is that feeling you would register at the end of ten or fifteen minutes of training. (It's true that if you continued at this pace long enough you would hit 20 on the scale, but that is not the point.) The 15 for interval workouts would be that perceived exertion at the end of an interval, or at the top of a hill (if you were doing natural intervals).

To get used to the scale, the following procedure is recommended: Jog very slowly around a five-minute loop, take your pulse, and mentally register your feeling. Repeat, going at your distance training speed, take your pulse, and register that feeling. Repeat once more, going at top speed.

---

*From the Swedish Ski Association in Stockholm, Sweden.

Take your pulse. Your feeling should be 19 or 20 after this one!

In general, but not in all cases, the perceived exertion score multiplied by ten should give a good approximation of your pulse rate. However, the idea is to get away from pulse rates as soon as you get used to your different feelings.

The most important point in monitoring your exercise is to learn eventually to go as fast as you want to, as in training, and as fast as you can without going under, as in racing. If you get to the point in your exercising where you don't have to take times or pulse rates but can listen to your body and get all the necessary signals, you will have learned pacing. Even aside from the racing angle, this is a marvelous goal to shoot for when you think about it. You and your body are working together and controlling the pace. Not many athletes, including Olympians, can do this.

EATING

If you train during the scheduled race time, your diet and meal habits will also fall into place. What and when you eat are individual things. You need to sample different approaches to find out what works best for you.

Most experts say you should ski about three hours after your last meal, but if you remain active for those three hours, your body will run out of fuel. If you stay calm, everything will be fine. What works best for us is to eat an hour or so before long workouts, then start slowly.

What you eat depends on your lifestyle. We eat a pre-race breakfast that consists of a fair amount of protein, such as eggs. And we don't take a lot of vitamins or medication, because we believe that most Americans have a diet that is sufficient in all the food groups and vitamins. If you have questions about your diet, consult your doctor.

Another approach is called *carbohydrate-loading*. This is a controversial process used by some top endurance athletes. Here's how it works. For three days, exercise to your exertion point, and eat foods low in carbohydrates for a day or two at this time. Doing this will deplete your carbohydrate stores. For the next three days, stop exercising and eat foods rich in carbohydrates. The theory is that your body will then store a more-than-usual amount of energy.

Many skiers who have tried carbo-loading have found that the mental pressures involved aren't worth the questionable benefits. Slight changes in body chemistry, such as those resulting from carbohydrate depletion, often cause depression or irritability. Part of the pressure results, of course, from sitting at the table eating displeasing food while everyone else is munching goodies. You should not try this regimen for the first time just before a race. Test it out during training to see if you feel any benefit.

In the continued effort to stimulate race day conditions, practice eating during your workouts. We recommend liquids containing sugar or glucose, and possibly some minerals. (See the "Liquid Thoughts" section in chapter 4 for more information.) Carry them in your fanny pack. If you know the race course and the location of food stations, use your pacing goals to figure out when you should eat during training. There may be a stretch on the race course with no food for 15 to 20 km—simulate it and see what happens.

CLOTHING

The clothing you wear during race day will be an important factor in your success (also see chapter 7). This doesn't mean you need to wear fancy garments to race or train. You just need to be reasonably warm, dry, and

---

Short Circuit Shorts

In colder climates, autumn and winter joggers often dress in sweaters, shell parkas, knit caps, gloves, and shorts, leaving their legs bare. The cold stimulates the legs, they say.

At best, the practice of being one-third naked in cold weather is uncomfortable; at worst it's downright dangerous. The "vitaliÆng" tingle of the skin that shorts-clad joggers speak of is actually numbness. Skin sensitivity decreases radically as temperature drops. Muscle sensitivity, which determines the ability to perform coordinated motion, falls even more rapidly, and is essentially nil at a muscle temperature of 15°C (60°F). This is why accident rates for certain types of manual work increase as temperature decreases.

Exercising with cooled extremities may also lead to internal problems. The body automatically reduces blood flow to cooled extremities in order to cut heat loss. But exercise increases heart rate and stroke volume, which increases blood flow. The combination of reduced blood flow to the extremities and increased blood output from the heart increases the amount of blood and blood pressure in the torso. The increased internal fluid pressure is sensed as a signal to urinate. This is why underclothed joggers and skiers find themselves running for facilities or trees more frequently than normal. Some think that the increased need to urinate is a result of having drunk too much before exercising, so they cut down on liquid intake. That only leads to decreased physical performance and possible dehydration. Others feel that they may be afflicted with an internal medical problem and go to their doctors, who, when they have the patient inside and warm, find nothing wrong. Some try to ignore their body's signals, believing them to be false alarms, and continue to exercise with the discomfort of an apparently full bladder, which hampers performance.

This is why prudent racers don knickers and knee socks for on-foot training whenever the temperature (including wind chill) drops below a comfortable level. In any case, the guideline is: When in doubt, overdress. It's always easier to take off a garment and tie it around your waist than it is to find more clothing when you're out running.

comfortable. If you are too cold or affected adversely by cold winds, you could be in serious trouble. If you are too hot, you will perspire too much. So, while training, work on various combinations of clothing. Wear long underwear that wicks perspiration from your body as well as some outer garments that help to evaporate perspiration *and* keep you warm. Take an extra hat or headband along and switch, as you would during a race. A good place is at the top of a long downhill, because on the trip down, a wet hat or headband could freeze right to your head and ears. Or try twisting the wet hat or band slightly on your head—that helps to bring drier parts of it in contact with the sections of your head that tend to cool the most. You may also want to put your hat and gloves on and off several times, depending on the wind chill factor. (Remember, when you ski down a hill, you develop your own wind chill.)

Once again, the idea is to learn to predict clothing conditions on race day by testing your predicting abilities in training.

THE FINAL TWO WEEKS

If you want to go the whole route on this preparation business, plan one final workout, perhaps a week before the big event. If getting to the race means rising at 4:30 A.M. and eating breakfast, then you should do that. We know competitors who rise early and then sit around to simulate a car ride. Then they go out and start waxing about an hour before their workout. They take food along in thermos bottles and ski nearly the whole race course distance, but at a slower, easier pace. Doing this once before a race, even if you have done the times and distances in previous years, still builds added confidence. It's enjoyable as well.

The best thing you can do during the last week is avoid hard workouts—not only because of the rest you'll need for the race, but also because of the disruption of traveling there. You're kidding yourself if you think you can gain some training effect at this date. If you have taken your long workout the week before the race, you will need a couple of days to recover. From then on, just ski easily. Wind down. Move more slowly.

MORE INFORMATION

Thousands of doctors are studying sports physiology, and during the past ten years or so there has been a wealth of information available. We've seen some trends come by once or twice and are not surprised at what we hear these days. We do have faith in the human body and feel that most people have not come close to reaching their limits of conditioning. We also believe that peoples' capacities for conditioning will improve in the coming years.

3
ROLLER SKIING

If you are serious about racing, sooner or later you will probably roller ski. You don't *have* to roller ski to race well. And even the most avid of roller skiers admit that it is, well, just a bit boring. But nothing beats roller skiing for simulating the real thing, especially for skiers who have no glaciers nearby for summer skiing or early autumn snows for pre-race training.

Skiing itself is by far the best training for racing. But roller skiing is a close second. So if you live far from the snow and are a ski-commuter, so to speak, then it's even more likely that you'll want to roller ski while in town.

If you're a serious racer who chooses only *one* type of training for off-seasons, you should try roller skiing. It's that good, and it even has an advantage over running: the movements are softer; they don't jar the legs and their joints.

There are many claims and counter-claims about how roller skiing started. Someone probably saw kids roller-skating and figured that with one or two adjustments, he could come up with a ski-like device for summer training. Just take a pair of sturdy cross-country racing skis with bindings, mount some ratcheted wheels that spin in only one direction, and presto, cross-country strides on asphalt! That, in fact, is just what the first roller skis looked like in the early 1960s. Järvinen wood racing skis had three wheels, one forward and two aft. Stories and then pictures circulated of Finnish racer Eero Mäntyranta using the things. Since Mäntyranta was the terror of the international racing tracks then, Finland was credited with starting the trend.

One glance at the world map provides a clue as to who are the most avid roller skiers: North Americans and Australians. The skiing populations in North America live farther south and have fewer glaciers and less early

Compared with today's roller skis, these 1960 models seem crude, but they do look more like skis. (Pietinen photo)

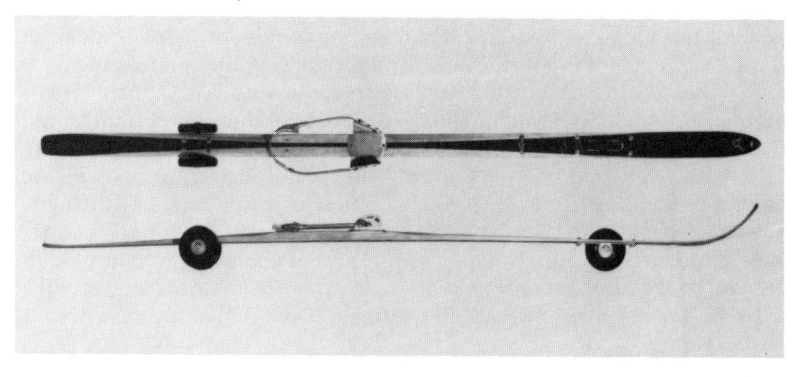

A rare early-1960s shot of Eero Mäntyranta at a roller ski race in Finland. (Pietinen photo)

snow than do their counterparts in Scandinavia and Northern Europe. And few Australians live anywhere near snow.

Roller skiing has been going on fairly steadily in North America for about twenty years. It's no new thing, and it does produce results.

Getting Started

Roller skis aren't cheap. A good pair will easily run you at least half again as much as a pair of top racing skis. And for roller skiing, you should have good poles with hard, carbide tips that don't wear on asphalt. That's another expense. So if you're still casual about racing, don't plunge into roller skiing unless you have plenty of cash.

As with snow skis, it's nice if you can actually test roller skis before making a purchase, just to see if you like and will be able to handle them. Be sure to get an idea of the cost and availability of replacement parts, since some parts are surprisingly expensive. If you get hooked on roller skiing, you will be wearing out tires, wheels, or bearings before too many months go by. (Some skiers on the U.S. Ski Team go through two sets of wheels a season.)

The diagonal stride and double-poling are the same on skis or roller skis. (Fletcher Manley photos)

Sooner or later you may have some mechanical difficulties, so when you buy skis it's a good idea to find out all you can about the workings of the moving parts. You can save time later by repairing your own skis, or putting on replacement parts.

Use regular cross-country ski boots and bindings. If you have some older, more rugged boots, you should use them because in roller skiing you'll have quite a bit of torque on your feet.

The bindings should be mounted where the manufacturer recommends. If there are no indications, then put the bindings on the balance point, as you would with a pair of snow skis. Caution: If you have a long ski boot, be sure the boot heel does not interfere with the action of the rear wheel. It might be necessary in this case to move the whole binding forward a bit.

Some skiers move their boots and bindings closer to the ratcheted wheel(s) than is recommended. However, too much dependence on these wheels that give you your purchase might lead to faulty technique.

You can use your regular-length ski poles for roller skiing, as long as they have hard tips. Some companies make special replacement tips for their ski poles because the tips will wear out if you ski very much. You may be inclined to use roller ski poles longer than your regular-length poles because the roller skis are platforms above the underlying surface. But remember, roller ski poles don't sink as do poles in snow, so you actually need the same length poles for both roller and snow skiing.

Until you become proficient at roller skiing, it's a good idea to wear long pants or warm-ups in case you take a spill.

If you are new to roller skiing, you should take it easy the first several times out. Fifteen minutes will do until you develop the knack and the muscle control necessary to ski.

Run a service check on your skis frequently. Keep them oiled, clean them if you have been out in the rain or if they are dirty, and by all means, check the nuts, bolts, screws, or whatever holds the wheels on. One of the unforgettable thrills in this sport is to lose a wheel on a fairly fast downhill stretch. It's an experience you can do without!

After you have skied a few hundred "Ks" you might check the wear on your tires. If you do a lot of snowplowing (see below), or ski hard on roads that are slightly crowned, you may find the tires are wearing unevenly. If so, switch your skis, left for right and right for left. If your bindings are 75 mm, they will also have to be switched.

Mild controversy surrounds the use of these skis as training devices for technique. One school of thought holds that the skis are best used for double-poling and that the diagonal stride should not be used unless it's absolutely necessary. The feeling is that you can build bad technique habits by skiing too much diagonal, because roller skis are not the same as snow skis. They are heavier and slower, and they never slip. We don't agree with this. We have found nothing more specific for training during the summer months (short of going to Australia for some snow skiing). It's difficult to believe that one might develop bad habits doing the diagonal, but not doing the double-pole.

Generally, roller skis are excellent for double-poling on the flats and doing the diagonal on uphills. On downhills, it's better to take your skis off and walk, until you are sure of yourself. Try to find a route with no fast downhill sections, and you will be happiest.

As you improve, you may find it possible to slow down on these hills by doing a bit of snowplow. This does not help with the wear and tear on the tires, wheels, and bearings, but it does slow you down. Most good skiers use this method for slowing down rather than taking off their skis and walking.

There are a few drawbacks to roller skiing, some of them humorous, some of them not surprising. It's possible to suffer from sore elbows because of

Early U.S. roller skiing: Mike Gallagher, then on U.S. team, now national coach, skiing on Vermont summer asphalt in 1967. (Michael Brady photo)

the jarring they take when you pole on pavement. If this happens, you will have to slow down or stop.

Some towns have ordinances pertaining to the use of skateboards on their streets and a few eager law enforcement officers can make life miserable for roller skiers. There are plenty of stories circulating about the legal interpretations or definitions of roller skis. Are they skateboards? Should they be registered? If they have brakes, are they in a vehicle class? Should they be classed as scooters? So far as we know, no town has specifically banned the use of roller skis, but the time may not be far off.

Motorists in roller ski areas are usually understanding when they see someone out training, but be careful—some people have never seen the things! There is some concern regarding which side of the road roller skiers should use. We suppose the legal beagles will come forward someday and tell us where we should ski, if at all. For now, though, we ski with the traffic. Of course, the best way to beat the traffic problem is to avoid it completely.

Top on the citizens' race circuit in 1981, Finn Pauli Siitonen shows a good diagonal stride on roller skis, using poles wound with reflecting tape for safety after dark. (Exel photo)

In some major cities, roller skiers use asphalted bike paths or closed parkways. There are even roller skiers in Central Park in New York City. About the best urban trick for roller skiing comes from California, where shopping center parking lots can be immense. Instead of early morning joggers there, you have early morning roller skiers.

As with all fast-developing sports, there are a few controversies in the roller ski world. Skis and methods for training with them are still developing. Theories abound, but basically it's a fine form of exercise, and quite safe if you take logical precautions.

4
THE INNER RACER

Citizens' races have so many grades of difficulty that it is impossible to set up rules as to who should race or to predict how well any one person will do at it. There are shorter events that almost any recreational skier can manage with little preparation and there are events for handicapped people; there also are ultralong races with profiles that only the best-prepared skiers should attempt.

So when advising people who are contemplating racing, we usually consider three general guidelines: health, fitness and training, and skill, in that order.

HEALTH

If you have no previous experience in racing or a correspondingly strenuous endurance activity, your first question may be, "Should I start racing?" The answer depends on your present physical condition and on your medical history. In general, if you are under thirty, have never smoked, are not overweight, and have a good medical history, you can probably start training for racing. But if you are over forty, overweight, a smoker, or have had any heart, lung, or other serious ailments, or even if you're simply in doubt about your state of health, you should consult your physician. Some races require that you have a medical checkup the same season that you race.

Your experience in physical activity also affects your health as a racer. If you have been physically active all your life, then you are probably prepared to meet the demands imposed by training and racing. This, by the way, is what's behind those stories you may hear of so-and-so who took it up a few seasons ago, and already places in the top quarter of the result lists. Look into that individual's background, and you'll undoubtedly find years of backpacking, hiking, mountaineering, canoeing, cycling, or other physical activities that require endurance.

If, on the other hand, you've led a sedentary life up to now, no amount of training, no diet, and no form of preparation or treatment will afford you the same physical potential as would have been possible had you been physically active all those years. Although there yet are no conclusive statistics on the subject, several medical reports imply that racing may be risky for those who start late in life and aim too high, beyond their capabilities. The message here is: Be realistic in your racing goals. Remember, most of those people you see racing well into their fifties and sixties have been doing it, or something similar, all their lives. So if you're of their age class but lack their background, settle for a lesser goal than beating them at their lifetime game.

Rutledge Gish. (Michael Brady photo)

Zooping Along

He got his first pair of skis for Christmas. That was in 1977, and he started skiing the following year. That alone was some task, as he lives in Fulton, Missouri. The next year, in 1979, he skied on the Tasman Glacier in New Zealand. And one year later, he took up cross-country ski racing, starting in the forty-five and over age class. He came in next to last in his class, but was so encouraged that he made citizens' racing his hobby.

Not bad for someone over forty-five, but notable for someone more than old enough to be the parent of someone over forty-five. For Rutledge Gish was seventy-one when he first tried citizens' racing. "They say the U.S. doesn't have any good old people, like Scandinavia," he remarks, "and I think it's nice to disprove that."

Once a cattle farmer, then a surgeon, and now a general practitioner, Gish knows well the benefits of exercise. What most folks his age don't realize, he feels, is that "it's great to be still learning."

For races he wears warm, comfortable farm clothing, which "doesn't scuff an old man." Before a start, he assiduously studies the course profile and marks all steep downhills on a course map, which he wears pinned to his left sleeve. "Got to know where they are," he says, "because they're my weakness. Otherwise I just zoop along."

FITNESS AND TRAINING

Besides being healthy enough to race, you should be able to go the distances involved to your own satisfaction. You are really on your own when assessing your capability and preparedness. If, say, you enter a citizens' race just for fun and know from experience that you can ski the distance involved, then tour away. But it's another matter if you aim to place well or want to try to win your class. As a general rule, as mentioned in chapter 2, you should be experienced in skiing at racing speed over the distance you intend to race. But there are exceptions, such as for some 80-km-plus races, where training over the full race distance is impractical for many skiers and impossible for most, because there just aren't that many long, prepared trails around. So, you should be able to move under your own power, on foot or on skis, at about the same speed as you intend to race. Train for a period of time at least equal to the time you think it will take you to ski the course.

An early start in citizens' racing: children at the start of the 1.2-km mini-citizens' race, Childrens' Championships Day, 1982, Oslo, Norway. (Michael Brady photo)

SKILL

Skill in racing isn't just the skill with which you execute the various maneuvers of skiing. It's also related to how well you ski at speed for a longer period of time. In racing, technique and level of training are inseparable, and perhaps best evaluated in terms of speed. Racing makes the most sense if you move at well above touring speed. In most citizens' races, a time equal to the winning time for a class plus 20 to 30 percent is regarded as good, and is usually recognized by the award of a certificate or badge. In terms of current race finishing times for adults up to about fifty years old, this means you should be able to ski a course similar to the one you intend to race at a speed of 9 to 11 km an hour or faster. Twice the winning time in any class is slow skiing.

Fitness and skill, the decisive capabilities once you have a clean bill of health, are related to and dependent on training (see chapter 2) and skiing technique (see chapter 5). These things depend on the way your body functions.

Running ski trails is one of the best forms of all-around off-snow training, as it involves both aerobic and anaerobic exercise. (Frits Solvang photo)

One of the factors that makes today's racers better than those of yesteryear, and makes training more efficient than it once was, is that more knowledge is now available on how the human body works when racing. Cross-country skiing at speed places premiums on efficiency of movement and on overall physical fitness. We'll say something about each one of these topics in this chapter. (For more information, see "Recommended Reading.")

THE OUTSIDE VIEW

There are two types of efficiency: the type you can see directly (or on video or in slow-motion movies) by watching a racer, and the kind you cannot see, which goes on inside the racer.

As a racer, your greatest concern should be the efficiency of your diagonal stride, the maneuver you use most often. Just how important is that all-important kick of the diagonal stride? What are the trade-offs? What are the penalties for a poor kick?

For the answer, we turn to a scientific field called *biomechanics*, and to some scientific work that was done for the sportsmedicine activities of the U.S. Ski Team a few years ago.

Let's say you are watching a race and are trying to find out just why the skilled racers ski faster than the average racers in the race. The U.S. Ski Team sportsmedicine researchers did just that. They took precise slow-motion pictures of racers racing, and measured speeds, stride lengths, and stride rates (tempos) of a large number of racers. Here is what they found (measurements are in the metric system, as is common in science and skiing)*:

Skiing speed = length of stride × stride rate (tempo)

Racers:	Speed, m/sec	= stride length	× stride rate
Skilled	4.64	= 2.88 m	× 1.61 strides/sec
Average	3.51	= 2.22 m	× 1.58 strides/sec
Difference	1.13 (4 kph)	0.66 m	0.03 strides/sec

Skilled racers had speeds of 16.6 kph (10.4 mph), while average racers were slower at 12.6 kph (7.9 mph). The 4-kph (2.5-mph) speed difference came mostly from the longer lengths of the skilled skiers' strides; the tempos, or how fast the skiers strided, were about the same. The skilled skiers got their longer strides by kicking harder, *not* by hanging onto their glides longer.

More research is now being done, so more results will probably become available. But for the time being, there you have it in numbers: if you want to ski faster, kick harder.

---
*C. J. Dillman, D. M. India, P. E. Martin, "Biomechanical Determination of Effective Cross-Country Skiing Techniques," *Journal of the United States Ski Coaches Association* (Winter 1979): 38-42.

THE INSIDE VIEW

Cross-country ski racing, like other endurance events, essentially requires the body to consume oxygen from the air and "burn" processed food to fuel motion. The processes involved are called *aerobic* (from the Greek, meaning "with air"). *Aerobic capacity* is an individual's ability to function as an aerobic machine.

Comprehensive physical measurements have shown that cross-country ski racing requires the greatest aerobic capacity of all sports, ahead of distance running, cycling, and swimming.

This means that if you do well at another competitive endurance sport, be prepared to do comparatively less well or to increase your training to do as well in cross-country ski racing. On the flip side of the coin, of course, is the benefit: cross-country skiing is perhaps the best all-around aerobic conditioner.

The aerobic processes can be summed up in a simple equation:

Fats, carbohydrates, proteins + oxygen = water + carbon dioxide + energy

Oxygen comes from air inhaled, and fats, carbohydrates, and proteins come from food consumed and processed by the body. Proteins are of minor importance in muscular work; their primary function is as a material for producing new muscle cells. Most of the muscular energy expended comes from oxidation of fats and carbohydrates. Each gram of fat burned produces about two to three times as much energy as each gram of carbohydrate burned. But the body's chemistry for burning fats is more complex, so the body almost always resorts to burning carbohydrates before fat. For most normal adults, the body's carbohydrate reserves will fuel about half-an-hour of fast skiing. Thereafter, the body gradually switches to burning its fat reserves.

The oxygen transport system includes the lungs, heart, and blood, where processes starting from inspiration and ending in oxygen delivery to the tissues occur. The capacity of the system is determined by the capacities of its component parts.

Lung Capacity

Lung capacity varies more than the capacities of any other oxygen-transporting organ. For average healthy adults at rest, lung ventilation — the amount of air expired per minute — is about 5 to 6 liters per minute. With each respiration, about 0.5 liter of air is inhaled and exhaled, and there are about 8 to 11 respirations per minute. With exercise, these numbers increase up to between 100 and 200 liters per minute for ventilation, 60 respirations per minute in rate, and as much as 3 to 3.5 liters in volume. But further increases are possible, so lung ventilation — or, as most people put it, just "breathing" — doesn't limit maximum oxygen transport.

Heart Capacity

Heart capacity also varies. The heart will pump about five liters of blood per minute for healthy adults at rest, up to a maximum of around forty liters for top athletes during exercise. Heart capacity is expressed in terms of *cardiac output*, or volume of blood pumped from one heart chamber per minute:

Cardiac output = heart rate × stroke volume

The *stroke volume*, or volume of blood pumped per heartbeat, can increase with training. The maximum heart rate is highly individual, but can also be increased with training. The average maximum heart rate is about 220 minus an individual's age in years. For instance, the average heart rate for thirty-year-olds is about 190 beats per minute. Well-trained individuals have greater oxygen transport capability than untrained people. This is chiefly because they have higher cardiac outputs, which, in turn, is mostly due to increased stroke volume. In these circumstances, cardiac output is maintained at a lower heart rate. This is why trained endurance athletes usually have lower resting pulses than average people. But the reverse isn't necessarily true: a low resting pulse is not necessarily an indication of physical condition or endurance capability. The limit of heart capacity is still determined by stroke volume and maximum rate—that is, how much the pump can pump, not its idling speed.

Blood Capacity

Blood capacity has to do with how oxygen is transported in the blood by bonding to hemoglobin, an iron-containing compound in the red blood cells. The difference in oxygen levels in the blood between that pumped out to the muscles through the arteries and that returned by the veins is called the *arterio-venous oxygen* (or *a-vO$_2$*) *difference*. This represents the oxygen consumed by the tissues. In trained athletes, it can be as high as 170 milliliters of oxygen per liter of blood, or 17 percent by volume.

Theoretically, there is some advantage to increasing hemoglobin levels in the blood. One gram of hemoglobin can carry 1.34 milliliters of oxygen, and the more hemoglobin there is, the more oxygen can be carried. This results in a bigger a-vO$_2$ difference. However, increasing the hemoglobin in the blood also makes it more viscous, which in turn makes it more difficult to pump. So there apparently are optimum hemoglobin levels, but as yet they haven't been determined. This may be why you hear so much about the role of hemoglobin in endurance events, and why theories abound as to the value of iron supplements or other dietary schemes to improve hemoglobin percentages.

Putting all the oxygen transport system factors into one handy formula gives the maximum transport and utilization, or *maximum oxygen uptake*:

Maximum oxygen uptake = heart rate × stroke volume × a-vO$_2$ difference

Well-trained cross-country ski racers have higher oxygen uptakes than average individuals, primarily because they have far greater stroke volumes and slightly larger a-vO$_2$ differences. In other words, both oxygen transport and oxygen consumption capacities are improved.

Anaerobic Processes

Although the body basically functions as an aerobic machine in cross-country ski racing, it cannot run on aerobic processes alone. This is because the aerobic processes are a bit lethargic in responding to demands for increased energy output, such as when you sprint at the start of a race or run up a hill. Aerobic processes work fine in what's called the *steady state* (condition of constant oxygen transport and utilization) but take up to three minutes to respond fully to demands for increased energy output. In these situations, the body calls on other, speedier processes that are termed *anaerobic* (without air) because they function without oxygen supply. The fuels for the anaerobic processes are carbohydrates that are stored in the muscles, which is why they are immediately available when needed. But they are small in quantity, so the amount of energy that can be delivered anaerobically is limited: the body cannot provide pure anaerobic energy for more than one minute. Anaerobic metabolism results in the accumulation of lactic acid, which can inhibit muscle performance and cause disagreeable sensations associated with going under, which racers talk about (see chapter 2). This is why the body usually works aerobically. Demands for sudden increases in power are met by an immediate burst of anaerobic metabolism, which is superceded as the aerobic metabolism builds up.

Negative Work

How active and how passive should you be in the various phases of cross-country ski maneuvers? Theories abound about the merits of *negative work*, the payback you theoretically get when running downhill (as opposed to running uphill, which takes positive work).

There are many ways to demonstrate that the body is more efficient at doing negative work than it is at doing positive work. In 1959, British scientist A. V. Hill described an experiment that illustrates the point:

> Two bicycles were arranged in opposition; one subject pedaled forward, the other resisted by backpedaling. The speed had to be the same for both, and (apart from minor loss through friction) the forces exerted were the same. All the work done by one subject was absorbed by the other; there was no other significant resistance. The experiment was shown in 1952 at the Royal Society in London and was enthusiastically received, particularly because a young lady doing the negative work was able quickly, without much effort, to reduce a young man doing the positive work to exhaustion.*

---

*A.V. Hill, "Production and Absorption of Work by Muscle," *Science* 131 (March 25, 1960): 897-903.

Training on roller skis with a pulse rate monitor around the chest. (John Caldwell photo)

What It Means

If you want to race well, you need both aerobic and anaerobic metabolism. Your maximum oxygen uptake ability, or maximum aerobic capacity, is what enables you to ski fast throughout a race. Your anaerobic metabolism is the reserve that enables you to produce sudden bursts of power, as in a sprint at starts or finishes. If you follow the general training guidelines outlined in chapters 2 and 3, you can't help but enhance those capabilities. For building both aerobic capacity and anaerobic metabolism in the combination that you need for racing, nothing beats training in the same sort of terrain where you will race.

Knowledge of the various racing demands enables you to plan your training. If, for instance, you find that you "die" on hills when racing, then you should seek hilly terrain to run on next summer. If you find that you do fine at the initial sprints and on hills but simply cannot last the racing distances, you need to build aerobic power and should focus on more distance work.

A food station at the American Birkebeiner. (Tom Kelly photo)

LIQUID THOUGHTS

A higher energy output involves a higher body metabolic activity, which requires more water. You perspire at a rate related to your activity, not to how much you drink. In addition, in cold weather, racers inhale cold, dry air and exhale moist, warm air. The moisture exhaled by the lungs removes water from the body. So, whether you realize it or not, you can actually suffer greater liquid loss while cross-country ski racing than while exercising at a corresponding level in summer temperatures.

Aside from making you feel thirsty, liquid loss may cut performance. This is why you should always drink when racing or training. You will probably find that you simply cannot drink too much, and that it's all too easy to drink too little.

It makes sense to sweeten your drinks a bit, both to improve the taste and to provide more fuel in the form of glucose, for the oxygen-consuming processes that give energy. This is another one of those areas that isn't yet fully understood, so you'll probably hear many conflicting theories and claims as to what should be in the ideal drink. We'll simply state here a few facts about drinking when training or racing:

How much you drink is usually more important than whatever a drink contains.

The temperature of what you drink has little effect on absorption. But many racers find that cold drinks can cause stomach cramps. In general, the best temperature is the same as for baby formulas: body temperature or just below.

In general, drinks containing more sugars empty more slowly from the stomach. This is why you may feel nauseated if you consume too many of these glucose-sweetened drinks while racing. A full stomach and full racing speed don't go together. If, for instance, you double the glucose content from 2.5 to 5 percent, you roughly double the time it takes for the drink to leave the stomach. So you really haven't improved glucose availability by making the drink sweeter. All the various reactions and processes involved are highly individual. But, in general, a 2.5-percent sugar solution is adequate for maintaining blood sugar level under most average citizens' racing conditions.

Sugars in drinks are beneficial only after they have been processed in the body. The body processes almost all sugars in the same way at approximately the same speed. So, despite any advertising claims you may hear, no one of the many sugars on the market is superior to the others. Sucrose, glucose, and fructose, for instance, perform equally as drink sweeteners. Beware of claims for so-called "natural sweeteners," as they may be more highly processed than common table sugar.

Stock up on liquids before a race, but avoid overstocking sugars. Despite advertising claims of "instant energy" from sweet products, there is no such thing. But there is the reverse: excessively high sugar levels in the body two to three hours before a race may actually lower your blood sugar level to below normal. This happens because the body reacts to the excess sugar concentration by secreting insulin, which acts to deplete sugar level. In other words, consuming too much sugar robs you of blood sugar.

There is a common notion that salt should always be taken with liquids to replace salt lost in sweating. Actually, the salt content of sweat is less than that of the blood and other liquids inside the body, so when you sweat, you become "saltier." This is another good reason to maintain liquid intake. For most racing situations, the salt content of an average daily diet will suffice. But racing drinks should contain slight amounts of salt because it speeds stomach emptying and therefore makes the drink sugar content available more quickly.

Those are the basic facts about drinking when racing. Don't be overly influenced by what anyone else is drinking. If it's the right kind of drink and it tastes good, then drink it. Remember, it's primarily how much you drink that counts; sugar content, and then all of the other things, comes after.

Through the years, drink fads have come and gone. Past favorites have included coffee with sugar and milk, milk and honey, water sweetened with maple syrup, soft drinks including the carbonated colas, malt beverages, and fruit and berry juices.

Here is our basic international drink. It's the beverage that seems at this time to work best for most racers, and you'll probably find something like it at most major races. It's the basic 2.5-percent drink, and is easily brewed with common kitchen ingredients:

The Basic International Special

1 gallon water
⅜ cup sugar
1½ teaspoons* salt
lemon, orange, grape, or berry concentrate for taste
Mix well in a large container and heat to about 150°F. Pour immediately into thermos jugs. Allow drink to cool slightly in cups or drink bottles before serving.

*Level, standard U.S. teaspoons (48 to the standard cup measure)

In long-distance racing, you should drink or eat every fifteen to thirty minutes. Remembering the body's capacity for absorbing liquids, try to eat slightly less than 170 gr (6 oz) per stop. You'll find that's actually quite a mouthful.

One last word to the wise: Avoid alcohol while skiing. It only depresses body functions and dehydrates you more rapidly. Imbibe after the race if you wish, when you are comfortable and warm.

5
TECHNIQUE

One of the joys of racing is, of course, being able to get from the start to the finish in less time than others. But racing also has hidden benefits, joys other than just being fast. It can be a unique experience in cross-country skiing. Some skiers say it borders on the mystical; they have visions while skiing. Such experiences belong to the joy of getting it all together, of mastering both technique and tracks. The exhilaration cannot be matched, no matter how many trails, how many courses you cover in a season's skiing.

Attempting to ski fast is superb self-instruction in ski technique, because skiing at speed contracts the time available for each maneuver. This, in turn, sets a premium on smooth, efficient movement.

Racing is nothing more than a faster version of good, basic recreational skiing technique. If you already ski well, little more need be done to your basic stride repertoire. But when you ski fast, you'll find that you use energy rapidly, and that the penalties paid for inefficient movement are correspondingly high. Efficiency becomes more important as your skiing speed increases.

Technique, What's That?

In the mid-1960s, the sport in North America seemed divided. There was cross-country ski racing, and there was cross-country ski touring.

Those days are gone. Americans and Canadians race well internationally, and in Canada, more cross-country skis are sold than alpine skis. Since our friend Ned Gillette has traversed some of the world's toughest terrain while expedition skiing on cross-country gear, nobody doubts that cross-country skiing can and is done anywhere there is snow. There is a continuous connection from recreational and wilderness skiing to racing.

The current misunderstanding concerns technique. Many feel that there are two different techniques: racing and touring.

We don't agree. Tennis players know that what wins at Wimbledon is useful in a Sunday social match. And you don't have to be a whitewater expert to know that good kayak technique is useful for more than just racing. So it goes with cross-country skiing. The technique of racing is that of recreational skiing; cleaned up, made faster, and done in the right place.

Technique simply involves learning to do what you can already do, only better.

There is no one, correct technique for skiing at higher speed, no single approach to the efficiency it requires. Your speed-skiing strides and maneuvers are personal; speedy movement amplifies, rather than reduces, individual differences. So the faster you ski, the less you tend to ski like others. This means that you should never try to imitate another skier's technique, no matter how skilled and fluid it appears to be.

Good technique, for either speed or leisurely skiing, can never be defined easily because snow varies, and the tracks set in it are seldom constant. Course inclination varies. Even the best waxers are not always successful. The mule-like kick on a klister ski that speeds you along a hard, wet-snow track will land you on your nose if used in a loose, soft powder snow track. You may be able to sprint into a skating stride at the start of a long race, but when you are tired a few hours later, the same maneuver might cost you your place in the race.

So, your technique should suit the snow, the tracks, the terrain, and your own abilities. With so many factors involved, what is good technique? Here's one definition:

Good cross-country ski technique is a skeleton of no-waste movement, around which you build the body of your own skiing style.

This definition doesn't tell you how to ski well. But it does tell you what

---

On "Weight Shift"

Weight shift, we all agree, is part of skiing. But what is it? Ask a dozen skiers, and you'll probably get a dozen answers.

This is because the very word *weight* clouds the real picture. Everyday experience overflows with examples of apparent increases in body weight. Run on a soft surface, and you leave deeper footprints than you do when walking. Whenever you move in any way, even at a slow walk, dynamic forces in your motion allow you to assume positions that would be impossible if you stood still. This is why studio-posed ads of models in sports togs always look wrong: static stances cannot duplicate the positions of movement.

In cross-country skiing, even moderately skilled recreational skiers kick with forces of up to 25 percent more than their body weights. Racers' kick forces may be twice to thrice their body weights.

Weight is so familiar a term that its very use conjures up visions of what a scale reads. So in striving to weight a ski, skiers often stand directly over it, as if balancing in that position when standing still. This alone has ruined a lot of otherwise good technique because a sideways rump thrust wastes energy and contributes nothing to forward power.

But, since we cannot change the language, we're stuck with *weight shift* and *weighting* for terms. So we use them with the understanding that they are misused. When we say a ski is weighted, we mean that the skier has put all available downward forces on that ski.

not to think of in improving your skiing. Just as you might say that not shuffling is part of good walking, the skeleton rule of good technique can steer you clear of pitfalls.

For instance, not weighting your trailing ski is part of good technique for the diagonal stride. The instant during your forward leg swing when the trailing ski comes down on the snow is unimportant. In ignorance of this obvious principle, many instructors and coaches preach *level feet*, saying that the trailing ski shouldn't hit the snow before the feet are level, just prior to the kick on the opposite ski. This misguides skiers into bending their forward-swinging knee as if they were running on foot. The fault is so common that you'll even see it in ski magazine photos and ads placed by firms that should know better.

Complete weight shift onto the kicking foot in the diagonal stride is good technique. But the exact lateral position of the hip over the kicking foot is immaterial. A sideways hip-swing may look powerful, but it serves no useful purpose, other than perhaps being the most natural way to ski for persons whose body builds put a bit of waddle in their walk.

A powerful, rapid kick is part of good stride technique. The straightness of the kicking leg after the kick is finished isn't important. If you have made the most efficient use of your leg muscles in kicking, that leg will automati-

Check diagonal stride weight shift by watching from front. (Fletcher Manley photo)

cally straighten out, maybe only for an instant too short to be seen by the unassisted eye. But still many instructors and coaches yell "straighten that leg" to skiers, believing that what they see, or do not see, is the result of an inefficient kick. High-speed motion-picture camera studies of the technique of top international racers, taken at up to forty frames a second, often fail to show a single frame with the skier's trailing leg completely straight. Something that happens in less than 1/40 second definitely does not mean that you should resemble a strutting rooster while skiing.

Speed in cross-country skiing is a game of translating the energy you have available into forward motion. Any movement that does not result in forward power, however small it may be, subtracts from your overall speed. Repeated many times, wasted movement takes energy that could otherwise get you to the finish line more rapidly.

Hands and arms tend to lead the body in cross-country skiing. They aid your balance and, in the strides, set your coordination. So, rhythmic arm movements are essential to good stride technique. But any arm, elbow, or wrist movement that does not directly result in forward power is questionable.

In the 1960s, when many Americans and Canadians were exposed to top-level international cross-country ski racing, many top Scandinavian racers were lumberjacks. They skied with arm movements used in their daily work. They always looked as if they were chopping wood, arms crossing in front of their bodies as they skied. More than one coach fell for the maneuver, believing it to be the key to efficient pole-power. University team skiers throughout the continent were instructed to "wipe their noses" with their forward-swinging hands. At the time, few university ski team members were lumberjacks, so the maneuver was wasted.

In the late 1970s, many U.S. racers picked up the habit of flicking their wrists at the end of the pole push phase. The trick was picked up from international team members who had probably seen some Russians doing it. They said it was supposed to relax the arm. But if you have to bend your wrist consciously, then you must apply some muscle force, and applying muscle force is no way to relax. (Actually, the origin of the maneuver was probably a hangover habit from growing up skiing with poles that were too long. In Eastern Europe, young racers ski with gear on loan from their clubs, and only the largest of clubs can afford enough gear to suit all skier heights.)

Powerful arm movements, particularly the pull on the pole when the arm is in front of the body, contribute to forward speed. But neither the extended forward stretch nor the other extreme—the clipped, bent-elbow swing—is good technique. The straight arm, a sort of boardinghouse-reach on skis, probably comes from an attempt to imitate top international racers. Their arms are often straight at the start of a poling movement. But just as a briefly straightened trailing leg signifies a completed kick, a straight forward arm is the sign of the end of a rapid arm swing at high skiing-speed. It's not the same as swinging a straight arm up, march style.

The bent-elbow boxer stance probably originated with racers skiing on overly stiff skis. With skis too stiff for your weight and skiing ability, you tend to stomp, as if kicking your feet into the snow for purchase. In doing so, you don't have time to glide fully, and that chops off your arm movements. The only way you can then maintain decent racing tempo is to ski with arms flexed forward. However, women often ski with elbows slightly more bent than do men of corresponding body proportions because female forearms deviate more laterally at the elbow. (This anatomical sex difference is brought about by the so-called carrying angle, enabling the woman to carry her arms past her wider pelvis.) Some women racers compensate by bending their elbows slightly when poling. This brings the poles closer in to the body.

You can maximize downhill speed by minimizing wind resistance. But that doesn't mean you should go into a full egg-position tuck on all downhills. After Franco Nones of Italy won the 30 km, the opening race of the 1968 Winter Olympics Nordic ski events, his downhill technique was scrutinized and copied. Analyses of the race "proved" that he had won on the downhills. Downhill was then a neglected aspect of cross-country ski technique, and the attention it received was long overdue. But the following decade of overemphasis on downhill had its drawbacks. Racers found the static muscular stress of holding a full egg-position on many downhills often resulted in cramps that degraded their strides on the intervening flats and uphills. Replicating the stance of the alpine downhill racer, who trains for that position only and holds it for no more than a few minutes in a race, simply is not a solution for the cross-country racer.

And so it is throughout cross-country ski technique. The goal is always to ski fast, but there are many ways of doing that. The point is not to confuse

Speed in cross-country skiing is a game of translating the energy you have available into forward motion. (Joan Eaton photo)

the exact way any skier executes a movement with the underlying correctness of that movement.

Fads have come and gone in ski technique, and they will continue to do so. None of us can be immune to their influence. But you should have one simple goal for speed: The best technique is the one that gets you from the starting line to the finish line in the least amount of time.

THE SKELETON TAKES SHAPE

One way to learn good technique is to watch *many* skilled racers. Watch classified races, citizens' races, and TV coverage of foreign races. Watch with

> ### On Your Toes!
>
> It's the winning racers who evolve racing technique, so they are always watched and studied. At World Ski Championships and Winter Olympics, the 30 km is always the first event on the Nordic program, so what happens there often sets the tone of the entire meet. Franco Nones's win of the 1968 Grenoble Olympic 30 km focused attention on the importance of downhill technique in cross-country ski racing. Thomas Magnussen's win of the 1974 Falun World Ski Championships 30 km sparked the fiberglass ski revolution in cross-country.
>
> So when Russian racer Vjatsjeslav Vedenin won the 1970 Vysoké Tatry World Ski Championships 30 km by more than half-a-minute, the probing eyes of coaches and racers were upon him. What did he do? Two years later, in the Sapporo Olympics, high-speed movie cameras and video units were trained on Vedenin as he won the 30 km by close to a minute. Aha! Now those behind the cameras would know what he did, after just a bit of analysis . . .
>
> Vedenin was found to double-pole more than most racers. The films also showed that he rose high up on tiptoe just before planting his poles in each double-pole movement. That was it! Eureka! A generation of racers were up on their toes.
>
> There's no data from the 1970s to indicate whether or not tiptoeing double-poling racers ski faster than those who double-pole with their feet flat on their skis. (There were, however, a few instances of embarrassing falls during the period, as racers switching to the newer, snout-type racing boots and clip bindings went over on their noses in double-poling.) None of the serious analyses of the movement could prove its universal utility.
>
> Some racers now use it, and some don't. Most use it sometimes, but not always. But some coaches still teach it as if it were gospel. They shouldn't. It's just another component of individual skiing style. It helps some racers and hinders others. Tiptoeing is no cornerstone of good technique.

a purpose. Select one maneuver you wish to improve, and see how it is done by the best racers. Watch for the dictums of efficient movement that they obey. There are just a few principles of faster skiing.

First, top racers appear to stretch out more, and their arm and leg movements are more extreme. This is a *consequence,* not a *cause* of faster skiing. They kick harder with each stride; they do not take giant steps. Think about what you do when you want to speed up while walking: you don't stretch the forward leg out in front more. You push off, or kick more vigorously with each step. A more vigorous kick doesn't necessarily require more effort. On the contrary; if you put all of your energy into a rapid kick, your leg muscles have more time to relax during the rest of the stride. This is one of the fundamental truths of fluid skiing movement: Executing a movement poorly or incompletely often takes more muscle, and therefore more energy, than doing it well.

Second, efficient speed-skiing requires that your weight be well forward over your skis on uphills, downhills, and especially on the flat. In this position, all forces act more efficiently to push you forward. For instance, in the diagonal stride, even a slight backward lean or sitting position causes kick energy to be directed more upward than forward. That wastes energy. When the body is in the right place for efficient movement, it seems to hang in an inclined position with hips and trunk well forward, before and during each glide.

Finally, although skiing faster involves a higher tempo with more rapid arm and leg movements, those who do it well never seem rushed. But, as you may have discovered if you have ever jumped in a track behind a good racer and tried to keep pace by duplicating his movements, you may feel rushed. The most obvious indication of less skill in cross-country skiing is the hurried, staccato move. There's plenty of time to do everything completely, starting and stopping each move at exactly the right instant and blending all into the rhythmic whole of the maneuver.

SPEED UP, BUT FIRST...

If you run or cross-country ski just slightly better than others, you probably have experienced the drawbacks of an overly rapid speed-up. Let's say you are out jogging. You're warmed up and running well along a familiar route. You easily pass a couple of duffers ahead of you. You no sooner pass than one of them speeds up to hang onto you. You hear the clomping, the puffing and panting behind, and glance back at the churning windmill in your wake. You don't know whether to laugh or be angry, so comic, yet so annoying is the scene.

The point of such an experience is that if you want to ski faster, set things up to ease your task. Whatever you do, don't suddenly decide to ski faster when on a tour, and flail away at it. You would both degrade your technique and wear yourself out. There are easier ways of starting to ski faster. Here are four tricks-of-the-trade, the "secrets" that the world's top classified racers use to polish their technique:

- **Ski in a good track.** Make it easy. You'll learn more rapidly if all external difficulties are removed, leaving you to concentrate on your technique.

Diagonal stride. (Fletcher Manley photo)

When you have mastered technique, you can seek challenge in coping with different terrain or snow conditions. For polishing their basic flat-terrain technique, many skiers find that a track that slopes up just slightly is ideal for speed-skiing practice. Skiing the diagonal stride with the small resistance of a slight grade actually helps skiers learn speed-skiing, as they must continuously propel themselves and cannot glide ahead of their stride. Double-poling in the opposite direction in the same track adds a bit of speed to ease the practice.

- **Warm up well before you attempt to ski fast.** Warm muscles are more efficient and will respond more fully to the needs of speed. One trick many

---

Unmistakably You

Even among the most skilled racers, cross-country skiing style is individual. No two racers ski exactly alike.

The differences are particularly evident in the classic cross-country ski racing profile: the racer at full speed in the diagonal stride with arms and legs stretched out. In this stance, all body proportions, angles, and physical idiosyncrasies stand out. This is why you can quickly recognize racers you know when you have been around the sport for awhile. The face can be obscured, but you can still identify the racer. The stamp of that particular individual is there for all to see.

Every time you see a silhouette of a racer on a T-shirt, in an ad, drawing, or photo, ask yourself, "Now, who is that?" You will sharpen your eyes for detail and come to appreciate just how individual cross-country ski racing can be.

skilled racers use in practicing speed-skiing technique is to ski on a circular track or trail that takes about half-an-hour to complete. First they ski one lap to warm up, wearing a jacket or warm-up suit. Then they strip off the outer layer and ski the subsequent laps for speed.

- **Ski a lot, "listen" to your body.** Good skiing requires practice; motions become automatic only after you have done them many times. Ski as much as you can. When you achieve the harmony of good technique, your body will send signals: it feels good.
- **Get some feedback.** Have a skilled coach or instructor watch you ski and comment on your technique. Or take advantage of the age of electronics: watch yourself on video. Many club, school, and college teams, and better-heeled ski centers use video as a teaching tool. An evening spent watching yourself and your friends or teammates can be most instructive and often downright amusing. Whenever you use video, try to view it as soon as possible after you have skied for the camera. You will retain more that way.

FLAT POWER

The diagonal stride is so basic that it has become the very symbol of cross-country skiing. A skier, arms stretched fore-and-aft, glides on one ski with the other ski trailing. But many people find it difficult to perfect this basic maneuver. The underlying problem is usually a case of misdirected effort. Skiers frequently strive to learn a good diagonal stride by focusing on attaining a graceful, distance-covering glide, on duplicating the symbolic silhouette of cross-country. They do themselves a disservice because the glide, though beautiful to experience or observe, is a secondary feature of the diagonal stride. It's the kick, and the movements tied to it, that are fundamental. If you have a good kick, a good glide will follow. However, if your kick is deficient, a good glide is impossible.

There are just three basic, simple facets of a good kick. First, your kick, however powerful it may be, must occur just as your legs pass each other. This is the same timing that you use naturally in walking. Second, always kick completely; finish each movement. This is what puts your weight forward over your opposite, gliding ski. Finally, to master the first two aspects, your body must be in the correct position—right over your kicking foot. This is also the best position for efficient poling.

Here are a few tricks that will help your kick:

• **Think of a complete stride as starting and ending with a kick.** What happens between kicks, any glide you attain, is your reward for having started and finished the maneuver well.

• **Think from above.** Seeing things from above is like reading a road map: you don't actually see it that way when you drive, but the visualization gets you where you are going, better than any other method. So, when skiing the diagonal stride, think of the bird's-eye view, as shown on page 83. Do your arms and legs move as parallel as possible to the track? They should, since that's the way you are going. Is your body directly over your feet? It should be because kicks are then most effective.

• **Ski without poles.** If you have difficulty timing your kick correctly, ski pole-less for awhile. With one less piece of gear to think about, you can focus on the essentials of your kick.

• **"Tie" hands to tips.** Glance slightly downward as you ski, so your ski tips just come into your field of vision when they are forward. Watch a tip as it comes into view and eclipse it with the opposite hand that is swinging forward. "Tie" your right hand to your left ski tip, and vice versa. Feel the synchronization of the stride.

• **Think ski-striding.** When running, you must time your kick correctly with respect to your leg and arm swings. Think of that feeling as you ski. If you find the recollection vague, take off your skis and ski-stride up a hill on foot to get the idea.

ABOUT FORWARD DRIVE

Cross-country skiing involves both active and partially passive portions in each maneuver. Just how passive should racers be in order to move fast? Should cyclists pull on the pedal upswing (isn't that what the toe clips are for?) or just concentrate on pushing down? Should cross-country ski racers whip their arms and legs forward in the strides, or simply allow them to swing in a pendulum fashion? Should they have forward drive?

The answer to that question is *yes*. But what is forward drive? Get a dozen coaches and expert skiers together and have them watch a top international competitor ski. Then ask the group if that competitor has forward drive. You will get a dozen or more answers ranging from "sure does" to "not at all," and everything in between, such as "on the uphills but not on the flats." Forward drive is one of those nebulous terms, like "quality," that nobody can define exactly. Having said that, we'll now define *forward drive*, as we use the term in this book: In movements like the forward leg swing just before the glide of the diagonal stride, and the forward arm swing in the

Check for motion parallel to the track by watching, or at least thinking, from above. (Fletcher Manley photo)

diagonal stride and double-poling, *forward drive comes from not being passive about the movement.*

As you acquire the technique of speed-skiing, forward drive will come naturally. You will not have to think about it.

Try this simulation exercise: Stand still with feet together. Swing your arms forward and backward as you do when skiing the diagonal stride. Let your shoulders rotate a bit, as they should when you ski. Speed up and make your backward arm swing forcefully, until you feel as if you are skiing at racing tempo. Sink a bit in the knees as your arms pass your body; make it all feel real. Now, can you honestly say that you're not putting any effort into swinging your arms forward? As you forcefully swing one arm backward in the poling movement, you automatically put force into bringing the other arm forward. You cannot avoid the reaction; the muscles of your body work that way. The same thing happens when you run on foot: you cannot have a powerful backward thrust with one leg while the other loafs on its way forward. That is, not if you run with a conventional gait.

Up until a few years ago, we both wrote and spoke more about forward drive than we do now. That was because most of the skiing public, and many fledgling racers, had had so little exposure to top-level racing that they didn't realize that skiing fast required high tempo. They tried to speed up by lengthening their glides alone. We had to say something to get the tempo idea across. Getting that trailing limb forward faster was at that time the best convincer.

Good racing rates range from around 80 to 120 or more strides per minute. You cannot work your limbs that fast without automatic forward drive.

We offer one important caution: Beware of forward thrust; it is an evil undoer of technique. Most susceptible are those with long alpine skiing experience. In fast alpine skiing, the pole movement is a thrust, plant, and

Double-poling. (Fletcher Manley photo)

retract sequence. This can carry over into cross-country. If you are not careful, you will thrust your arm straight ahead, as if punching an imaginary boxing bag hanging just in front. It's so typical and so telltale a sign that for years, we've surprised first-time pupils in our ski classes by "knowing" that they came from an alpine ski background.

If your body position is correct for your skiing—just the right amount of forward lean for your speed, stride, the track, and the terrain—and your tempo is high enough to maintain forward momentum, you'll have all the forward drive you need. Think about it only if you find yourself slowing down and losing momentum between kicks.

DOUBLE-POLING

Most recreational cross-country skiers regard double-poling as an advanced racing technique. Myth surrounds the maneuver, especially since 1981 when Bill Koch set a new world's record for cross-country skiing speed using it (along with a lot of skating). Do it and presto! You have speed. But not always. Here are a few facts about the maneuver:

• Whenever your glide could get ahead of your stride, such as on slight downhills, double-poling is faster than diagonal striding. It's also faster if you've missed the wax and have slippery skis.

• When combined with in-track strides or skating steps (such as when changing directions to another track), double-poling accelerates. But it reaches a maximum tempo more rapidly than does diagonal striding.

• Contrary to popular opinion, double-poling is not a strong-arm maneuver. In fact, for a given body weight, it requires less arm strength than

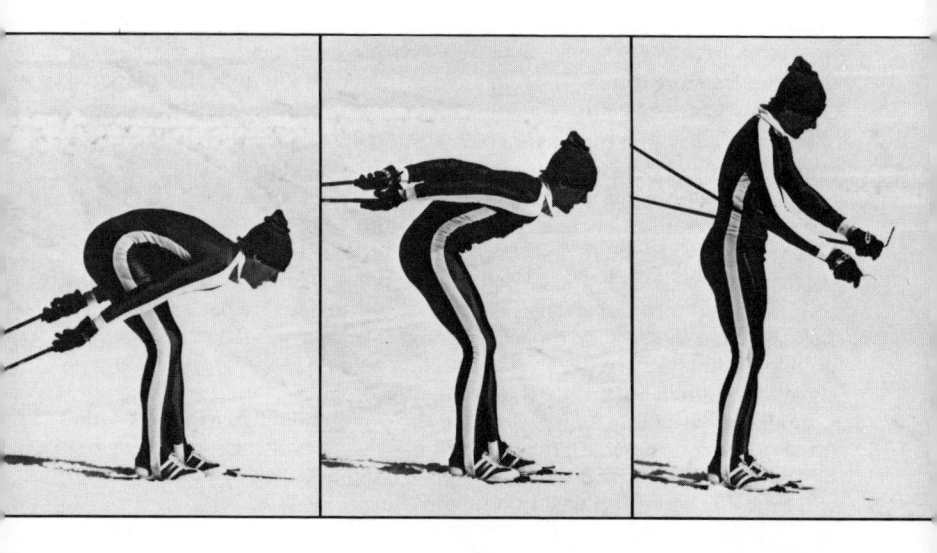

Double-pole stride. (Fletcher Manley photo)

does diagonal striding. This may be why top female cross-country racers tend to use it more than their male counterparts.

• Double-poling isn't just one distinctive maneuver. It is a spectrum of maneuvers executed to suit terrain, track, snow, and speed, as well as the racer. It is the cross-country skiing maneuver that is most individual. There's no way to say just when you should double-pole and when you should not. And what suits you may not suit the skier ahead or the skier behind.

• At racing tempos, there are two extremes of the double-poling maneuvers. In *straight double-poling*, with glide on equally weighted skis, forward push comes from the arms and upper body. In the *double-pole stride* or *one step*, a one-leg kick and a double-pole arm maneuver provide forward power. There are many variations between these two extremes. The kick may be short or long. The leg may swing back but not kick, as you arch over the poles for more thrust. The maneuver can lead into or out of the diagonal stride as you change strides.

• Many skiers and instructors practice and speak of two- and three-step double-poling. These maneuvers probably originated in the late 1950s and early 1960s with some Swedish woodsmen who were among the better racers of their time. Their technique was unusual, but their tough work backgrounds gave them the strength to go like the blazes. So others, particularly the Swedes and those influenced by Swedish technique, copied this inefficient technique. The slowness of the maneuvers has some utility, such as when racers wipe their noses or grab a feeding-station drink while double-poling. Otherwise, they are used so seldom that there's no point in considering them a part of stride technique.

In all double-poling maneuvers (we show here only two extremes—the no-step and the one-step), the key to fluid forward power lies in getting the most out of your trunk. If you have a good diagonal stride, your limb action will probably serve you well in double-poling.

The command is, "sink!" Once you have planted your poles, you should feel throughout the rest of the maneuver that it's your body weight sinking over the poles that thrusts you forward. Let your upper body drop until you feel it isn't practical to drop farther. Then straighten out your arms for the push past the knees to the rear.

Otherwise, the way you perform the movement is simply up to your personal skiing style. Some racers reach far forward with almost straight arms, while others have a slight bend at the elbow. Some drop their heads completely as if to examine the snow between their feet, and others cock their heads to see just a bit straight ahead. There are, however, two faults to watch for that detract from the maneuver's efficiency.

First, overdoing the backward pole push gives you almost no additional forward power. It pulls your trunk and arms so far back that you have to expend energy to get up from the squatting position. The telltale sign of overpush is poles swinging wildly up in the air behind, like a peacock tail trailing the skier. Remember, over 90 percent of the work is completed by the time your arms pass your knees; the rest is just frosting on the cake.

Second, some skiers sink their backs, while keeping rump and shoulders high as they pole. This is the swayback position, guaranteed to make your back sore. It also wastes arm power that is directed more up in the air than forward along the track. Remember, the commands for the back are "bend, straighten, bend, straighten."

The double-pole stride or one-step double-pole is a cross between double-poling (with no steps) and the diagonal stride. In this maneuver, timing is crucial to efficiency and power. The kick should be timed so the kicking leg is fully extended in back, just at the instant when the arms are fully extended forward, ready to plant the poles. From this stretched-out position, the body contracts and curls up toward a fetal position. The arms move backward and the trailing leg comes forward. It is the successive stretching and contracting that gives the stride its power.

Though it might be argued that the double-pole stride really isn't a stride, as one often does only one or two maneuvers at a time, we liken its leg movements to those of the diagonal stride with good reason: you should be able to kick with either foot. If you are one-sided in the maneuver, you severely limit its utility. In track turns, for instance, you are faster and more stable if you kick on the inside ski. If you can double-pole stride only with a kick on the right leg, you'll lose time double-poling in left turns.

SKATING AND CHANGING TRACKS

Plunk a small child down on skis without instruction, and it won't be long before you see some skating. Skating is a natural maneuver on skis. It is frequently used in racing for sudden acceleration or for rapid changes in direction.

It is best to use double-pole rhythm for the racing skate-stride, as shown in the illustrations of track change on page 89. But diagonal rhythm can also be effective.

THE MARATHON SKATE

A skating maneuver that is gaining popularity, especially on courses that have long flat sections, is the so-called *marathon skate*. Americans racing on a river course in Sweden picked up this technique and have been instrumental in spreading it around the world. The jury is still out—particularly in some of the more conservative countries such as Norway and Russia— trying to judge its effectiveness for races such as the World Championships and the Olympic Games, but meanwhile the North Americans are cruising ahead with it.

The skate is done by splaying one ski to the side, as in a regular skating stride, and pushing off it as you double-pole. The other ski is kept in the track. Repeat, splaying the same ski to the outside. After ten or twenty skates to one side, you will find it beneficial to switch to the other side.

The conditions of the snow just to the outside of the track often dictate which foot to skate with, and most skiers prefer skating off a slight downslope, assuming the snow is well packed. Strong skiers use this technique to go up slight hills as well.

THOSE UPHILLS

The 1936 International Ski Federation (FIS) competition rules state, "cross-country race courses should be so laid as to include approximately equal portions of climb, descent and level running."

Those rules are about classified racing, the stuff of Olympics and international championships. But they also have bearing on citizens' racing. Citizens' races are, after all, arranged on courses in the same terrain as classified races and sometimes along the same trails. What's true in general for

Change tracks in the diagonal rhythm. (Fletcher Manley photo)

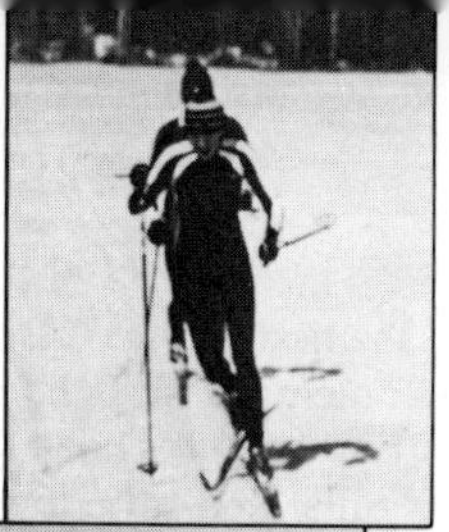
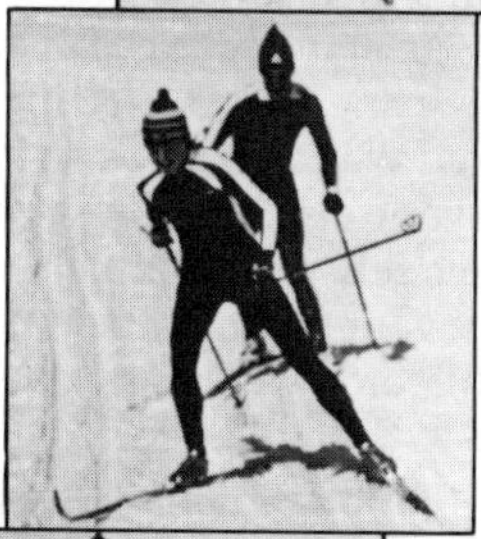
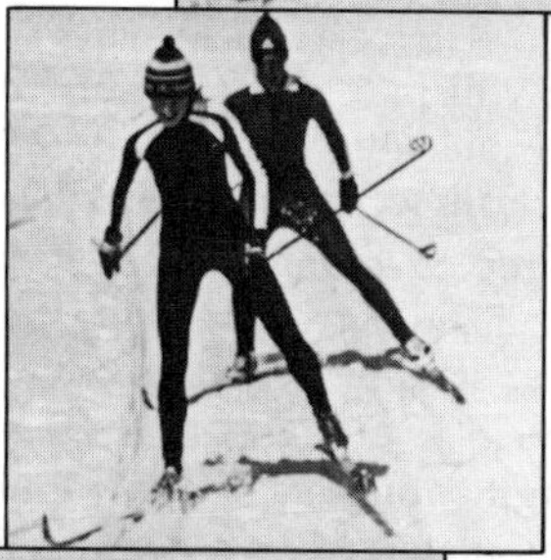
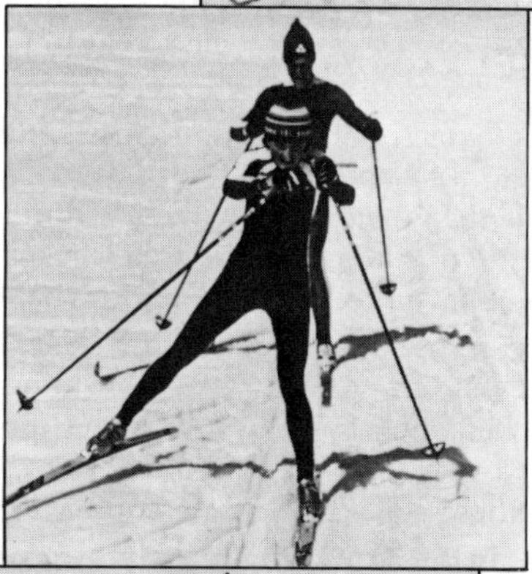
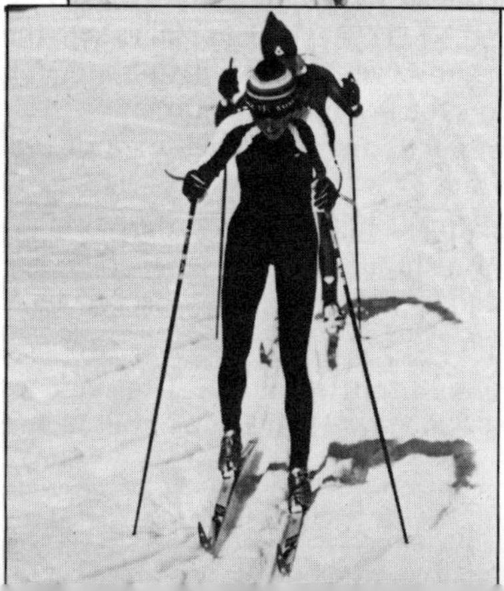

classified racing is also true for citizens' racing. In one respect, cross-country ski racing hasn't changed in fifty years: there are still a lot of uphills.

For years it's been said that cross-country ski races are won or lost on the uphills. Recently downhills have been in the limelight too. About a decade ago somebody noticed that a healthy percentage of winning racers' leads were gained on downhill sections of the track. True. But what was overlooked was that those winners also gained a bit, or at least did as well as everyone else, on uphills. The moral is simple: How well you do in a race is still largely determined by how well you do on uphills. Our message to all who want to race is *focus on the uphills.*

Hills are a challenge, not only because they are there, but also because the way you should attack them depends on many variables:

- **Stamina.** Skiing hills at racing speed is the physiological equivalent of sprinting. It forces you to work anaerobically (without enough oxygen), pushing you into oxygen debt. Your chance of success on hills depends primarily on your ability to sustain this type of effort. No matter how polished your technique, you will not get up the hill if you "run out of gas."
- **Incline.** Steepness dictates technique. Your skill, and some of the other variables listed here, determine how far you can diagonal stride up a hill of increasing steepness. But there comes a point where everyone has to herringbone.
- **Length.** You may be able to run a short hill at full speed, and pay back the accumulated oxygen debt on the following downhill. But on a longer hill, you'll have to pace your stride to get to the top still in a condition to breathe.
- **The track** (or lack of it). If you're lucky enough to be one of the first in a race to come to a steeper uphill with a good track, you may be able to diagonal stride the whole thing with ease. But if you come to the same hill with its upper two-thirds chopped to a soft mass by herringboning racers ahead, you will have no choice but to do what they did.
- **Your wax** (or the suitability of your waxless skis for the snow involved). The grip your skis have on the snow determines what technique you must use and how well you can ski uphill. With slipping, nongripping skis, you are limited to a very broad herringbone, or maybe even a sidestep. When forced to use these steps, you know you have washed out of the race.
- **The point in the race.** If you're tired toward the end of a race, you might want to let up on the hills, so you can still race to the finish. Early in a race, you may want to conserve a bit of hill-climbing energy for hills you know come later. Or if it's the last hill, and you know that the finish is just ahead, you may want to go all out and swallow your pride if you have to walk across the finish line.
- **What comes after.** A hill followed by a short flat and then another hill is double-trouble. You should regard it as a single hill. A hill followed by an easy, long downhill is a blessing; you don't have to work very much after you reach the top.

Hills set a premium on technique. Deficient technique on the flat or downhills makes you slow. With poor uphill technique however, you can stop dead in your tracks or end up in a heap on the snow.

There are so many ways to ascend a hill and so many different hills, that no one facet of technique can be singled out as the most vital. However, there *is* one prevailing principle of good technique: Weight over your feet.

If your weight is too far forward and you are leaning into or "clinging" to the hill, you are essentially pushing your skis back downhill. Unless you have super-sticky wax already well balled-up with snow, your skis will most likely slide right back downhill and you will end up on your nose.

When your weight is too far backward, your work load is multiplied considerably. With each step, you must hoist yourself up over your feet, as if you were trying to ascend a flight of stairs while sitting in a chair. The position may feel falsely secure, but it could bring you to a very rapid halt.

If you have ever climbed anything, from a rock wall to a telephone pole, you know the axiom of getting your rear out over your feet. That's what gives your feet the bite they need to support you as you climb. The same is true for skiing up a hill. Weight over your feet gives your skis the force they need for the grip that makes the ascent possible. But this does not mean you should squat or sit as you ski. Such positions, though erroneously still taught by some instructors and coaches, only make you work harder. To see why this is so, think of how much more difficult it is to pedal a bike while sitting on a seat adjusted far too low for your leg length than it is when the seat is at a more correct height.

There are two other general rules for uphill skiing. They both follow naturally if your weight is over your feet. First, you should keep your poles low and angled back so you can push efficiently. This is especially true on steeper uphills, where your glide may disappear altogether and amputate your arm swings to short strokes. Second, although your arms work harder on uphills than on the flat, it's still your legs that should do most of the work. Remember, you can always stand with feet together and pole yourself along a flat track, using double-poling or diagonal-poling movements. But unless you're built like a gorilla, you cannot do the trick uphill.

Uphill technique can be broken down into broad categories according to the incline of the slope. They are slight inclines or flat uphills, and steeper or "real" hills.

The borderline between the two is not exact; we simply cannot tell you that on inclines of less than X degrees you ski this way, and on those of more than X degrees you ski that way. True, nobody can ski up a vertical ice wall, and a flat is a flat. But between those extremes, the problems posed by an incline are relative. Full of vim and vigor, you may sometimes scamper up hills on well-waxed skis that otherwise, especially if you missed the wax, reduce your gait to a plod.

Slight Inclines

Use your normal flat techniques on slight inclines. Just put a bit more oomph into your strides to maintain speed. The diagonal stride, double-poling, double-pole stride, skating—all the flat techniques may be done on slight inclines.

Moderate uphill—stride little altered. (Fletcher Manley photo)

When skiing up long, gentle slopes, you will discover that your flat technique is put to the true test as you continuously work against gravity. But, remember, you can use gentle slopes to sharpen your flat technique. Find a slight incline where you ski. Ski it again and again, preferably throughout a season, in differing snows and track conditions. You'll soon discover what's right and what's wrong with your stride.

Steeper or "Real" Hills

This is what the FIS regulations mean when they speak of hills. This is where races are won or lost.

Common to all uphill racing maneuvers is the diagonal rhythm. It is usually executed with shorter strides and at a higher tempo than is the diagonal stride on the flat. We divide the maneuvers into three groups, according to where the skis are pointed in relation to the track: uphill diagonal strides, the herringbone, and the half herringbone.

Uphill Diagonal Strides

Skis are pointed straight ahead in the track (if the track is still there). Movements are modified versions of the flat-track diagonal stride. We have four variations: bounding, the shuffle or sneak, dogtrotting, and running.

- **Bounding: the power play.** Bounding is attacking the hill with all your resources, like sprinting a flight of stairs three at a time, or bounding uphill in the on-foot ski stride.

With your hips, knees, and ankles flexing, you leap up the hill, coming off the ball of your foot with each stride. Properly done, the bound is the fastest way to get up a hill. Even though you may not feel strong enough for the maneuver, it's probably already part of your skiing repertoire. How do you get over a foot-high rise in the track, such as at the edge of a road where the track has crossed at right angles? You probably put in one real good kick and leap up and over to continue your stride rhythm. That's one bound. Learning to put a few together will aid your racing technique, especially on those short uphills that otherwise break your rhythm.

- **The shuffle or sneak.** This is no pussyfoot stride, but rather a refined technique used by all good racers at one time or another. It is especially good on soft, powder snow or whenever grip is marginal. It can also be used on relatively steep, longer uphills. Delicately keep the ski in contact with the snow, doing as little as possible to diminish its chances of biting in. Do not drag your feet as if shuffling on foot. Descriptions of how it is done are as varied as skier experiences. Some say the foot comes forward like a Greek line dancer pointing a toe. Others say the foot comes forward like a cat's paw trying to push snow backward. One advantage of the maneuver is that it can be done at a very high tempo; you literally downshift gears, as you would on a ten-speed bike or in a car approaching a big hill.

Steeper uphill — the stride adapts. (Fletcher Manley photo)

- **Dogtrotting.** The dogtrot is a bouncy version of the diagonal stride, used on inclines where you get little or no glide. Most good skiers do it automatically and often. Think of what you do at home, in school, or at work when you're in a hurry to get from one place to another, separated by a couple of long halls and a flight of stairs. You walk the first hall rapidly. You get to the stairs. Toe on the first tread, and you go up with a quickened tempo. You get to the top of the flight, and walk quickly down the second hall. You've walked fast in the halls, but trotted the stairs.

Change Gears!

Just as race car drivers continually shift gears to get the most out of their machines, animals—including humans—are capable of instinctively changing their gaits to suit their speed. The goal for both machines and animals is the same: Maximum speed for minimum energy expenditure.

Horses are skilled at matching gait to speed. As they pick up speed, they change from a walk to a trot to a gallop. Walking requires a lot of leg motion for little ground covered and becomes inefficient when done rapidly. Trotting, with its bouncing motion, is more efficient. And better still is the gallop with two bounces, one with the front and one with the hind legs.

Humans, with only two legs, don't have that same range of gaits. Walking and running are the only basic human gait forms.

But on cross-country skis, we have a greater number of gaits at our disposal because poles are also used for locomotive power. Skilled cross-country ski racers continually match their stride length, tempo, and type to their speed, the terrain, and the snow. Like car drivers and horses, they change gears.

You can raise your tempo and make your strides as short as you like when dogtrotting up a hill on skis. The movements don't have to be complete; there is not as much time available for each step as there is in bounding. You don't have to come off the ball of your foot or pole powerfully, either. Just keep trotting. Think of the dog.

- **Running.** To be truthful, skis and poles do slow you down on steeper uphills. If you could somehow get the same support underfoot as the ski affords, you would be faster running up the hill on foot. This, by the way, is why cross-country ski racing times are not astonishingly better than cross-country foot running times. Skiers are faster on downhills and some flats, but runners are far faster on uphills. This is why many racers apparently forget the refinements of ski technique and jog or run up hills. It's not a beautiful maneuver, and it takes muscular power and suitable conditioning (anaerobic capacity) to perform well. But nothing can beat it for speed. The idea is to run hard enough to punch your skis into the snow for good wax bite, but not so hard that they dig in and slow you down. Keep time with your arms and maintain diagonal rhythm, but you don't have to push hard because it's your legs that do most of the work. You may even find yourself poling a bit wildly for balance, as running is a bit rougher than smooth diagonal striding.

The Herringbone

Skis are pointed outward, tips spread and tails together. The maneuver is named for the pattern left in the snow. The herringbone is the standard last resort in racing. If it doesn't work, you're no longer in the race.

In some circles, there seems to be a stigma attached to the herringbone, and "experts" of those groups pooh-pooh the maneuver, deriding it as a beginner's step. True, skilled racers often can do an uphill diagonal stride while those with less skill have to herringbone. But that doesn't detract from the utility of the maneuver. Together, we've seen major international classified and citizens' races on four continents, including all World Ski Championships and Winter Olympic Games for more than a generation, and we've yet to see a major meet in which the herringbone was not used. It's a reliable stride and, when done well, an amazingly fast way to ascend a steeper hill. There are a few tricks to doing it well.

First, stand up well over your skis, but do not lean forward from the waist. The herringbone unfortunately gives a false sense of stability that leads to weighting errors. Remember, speed is your goal in racing, so the more you have to move in a maneuver, the more energy you waste.

Second, take lots of smaller steps, change gears, and up your tempo. Giant steps work against you (try a few oversteps to see why). The rhythm is diagonal, in the pace of an uphill run.

Finally, practice switching in and out of the herringbone. This is where many racers lose time. They come almost to a standstill and get into a static herringbone position. Then they start up again, reverse the procedure, and change back to the diagonal stride at the top of a hill. Get into the herringbone before you really have to use it, and take just one more step than you really need before changing back to another stride. In a race, there's no pride in leaving that straight track everywhere you go.

*Herringbone — for steeper hills.
(Fletcher Manley photo)*

*Herringbone — the usual view.
(Fletcher Manley photo)*

The Half Herringbone

One ski is pointed outward in the herringbone position, while the other is pointed straight ahead in the track. Done using uphill diagonal stride technique, it's lopsided and not very pretty. But whenever straight uphill diagonal striding is marginal, the half herringbone is far faster than the full herringbone.

Let's say that you're skiing in the track up a hill, and suddenly one ski slips. Maybe you're too tired to punch that ski down into the snow for good grip, or maybe you're not waxed right for the hill. In any case, there you are, one ski and one pole in contact with the snow, rocking forward as that slipping ski shoots out from under you, back down the hill. You've still got some forward speed, but now your rhythm is broken, or so you think. The trick is to stay stable on the opposite ski, keep your rhythm, and bring the offending ski forward, up and out of the track. Tip it out in a half-V position. Keep going upward using the half herringbone. Chances are you'll be able to keep the other ski in its track. If it also slips, you'll have to resort to the full herringbone. Practice the half herringbone on hills where you feel secure. Get the feel of doing it on each side. In races, you'll find it especially useful whenever courses wind up gullies, and tracks drop off to one side. That's the side for the half herringbone.

The half herringbone —for uphill speed. (Fletcher Manley photo)

DOWNHILLS—THE FINAL FINESSE

On the recreational skiing scene, cross-country downhill has recently blossomed into a "new" form of skiing. It even has books, lingo, and its own races. To those who were around the North American skiing scene prior to World War II, it amounts to nothing more than a rediscovery of alpine skiing in the 1930s, before that sport grew and became more specialized.

Today, racers still win basically on the strength of their uphill and flat terrain capabilities. A good downhill technique is simply the final finesse. More racers now realize that downhill polish is attainable, but that realization has both merits and drawbacks. The advantage is that improvement on any part of a course will improve overall time. One major disadvantage, though, is that excess attention may be focused on downhill technique at the expense of training for flats and uphills. With this caution, we mention the facets of downhill technique important to cross-country ski racers.

First, cross-country downhill races are run mostly in tracks. Your downhill ability is determined by your skill in feeling tracks and in feeling comfortable with downhill speed.

If you feel weak on downhills, no minor adjustment in your technique will aid you as much as skiing more downhill. Get the feel of how to weight your skis, and how to react to small bumps and dips in the track. With experience, speed becomes less frightening.

Body position is crucial on downhills. For stability, your weight should be as far forward as is comfortable on most downhills. For more speed, shift

*The snowplow—a safe stop.
(Fletcher Manley photo)*

(Top, left) *The erect stance is the most stable.*

(Top, right) *The crouch cuts wind resistance.*

(Bottom) *The egg for maximum speed. (Fletcher Manley photos)*

your weight back just a bit. Hands and arms should be low to lead your body down the track. Most critical are your knees ("Skiing is kneeing" the Austrian instructors in New England used to say). They are your steering; where *they* go, you and your skis follow. They are also your shock absorbers. For that reason they should be treated with respect. They're not as flexible toward the end of a race when you may be tired, as they are when you're fresh.

Resistance works against you. If you've waxed well for the course, wind resistance is the major braking factor in downhill speed. You may scoff at the thought since cross-country skiing speeds are relatively low. But think of pedaling a bike against even a moderate breeze. If you sit erect instead of hunched over the handlebars, you have to work harder to maintain speed. Likewise, when skiing downhill at even moderate cross-country skiing speeds, you can cut wind resistance by streamlining yourself. A tuck is a good, stable position for most downhills. The extreme-egg, as used by downhill ski racers, is fine on a perfect track. But if the track demands control, or if you are too tired to hold a deep tuck position, you're better off higher up. In others words, do cut wind resistance, but not at the expense of being so unstable that you lose control and have to bail out of the track.

Finally, you should relax and rest as much as possible on downhills. If you find yourself straining to hold the track or your position, then you are sacrificing performance on flats and uphills for the slight gain you may have on that downhill. Some racers like to hyperventilate (breathe in and out deeply) on downhills. Others aim for total relaxation while they are still in motion. One favorite relaxed position is a good tuck, with the forearms resting on the thighs. Your hands should be just slightly ahead of your knees, with poles aimed straight back and tucked between the upper arms and the torso.

HOW TO BE GOOD AT POOR SKIIN'

Many alpine and wilderness skiers think there's little challenge in track skiing. After all, they contend, "Aren't tracks always the same?"

It won't take much track skiing for you to discover the error of this view. As soon as you start to ski fast in tracks, you will realize that no two tracks are the same. After a bit of racing, you will become accustomed to assessing the characteristics of tracks at the time you ski them. What, for instance, have the sun, wind, and temperature changes done to he morning's good tracks? Will racers ahead of you wear, or polish, the tracks? What about falling snow? Rain? Condensing fog? The variations are endless.

Other things equal, the racer who masters the greatest spectrum of snow and track conditions is the racer who most consistently ends up toward the top of the result list. Mastering different track conditions is mostly a matter of perception, of being able to detect what's underfoot and ahead, and modifying your technique accordingly. The kick that's great on a hard track will leave you wallowing in softer, powder-snow tracks. The downhill that's a cream puff when there's powder on it may be a real hair-raiser if the tracks are glazed and frozen.

You are completely on your own, for the feedback you get from a track and the way you react to it is a personal thing. But a few guidelines follow.

Skating turn downhill. (Fletcher Manley photo)

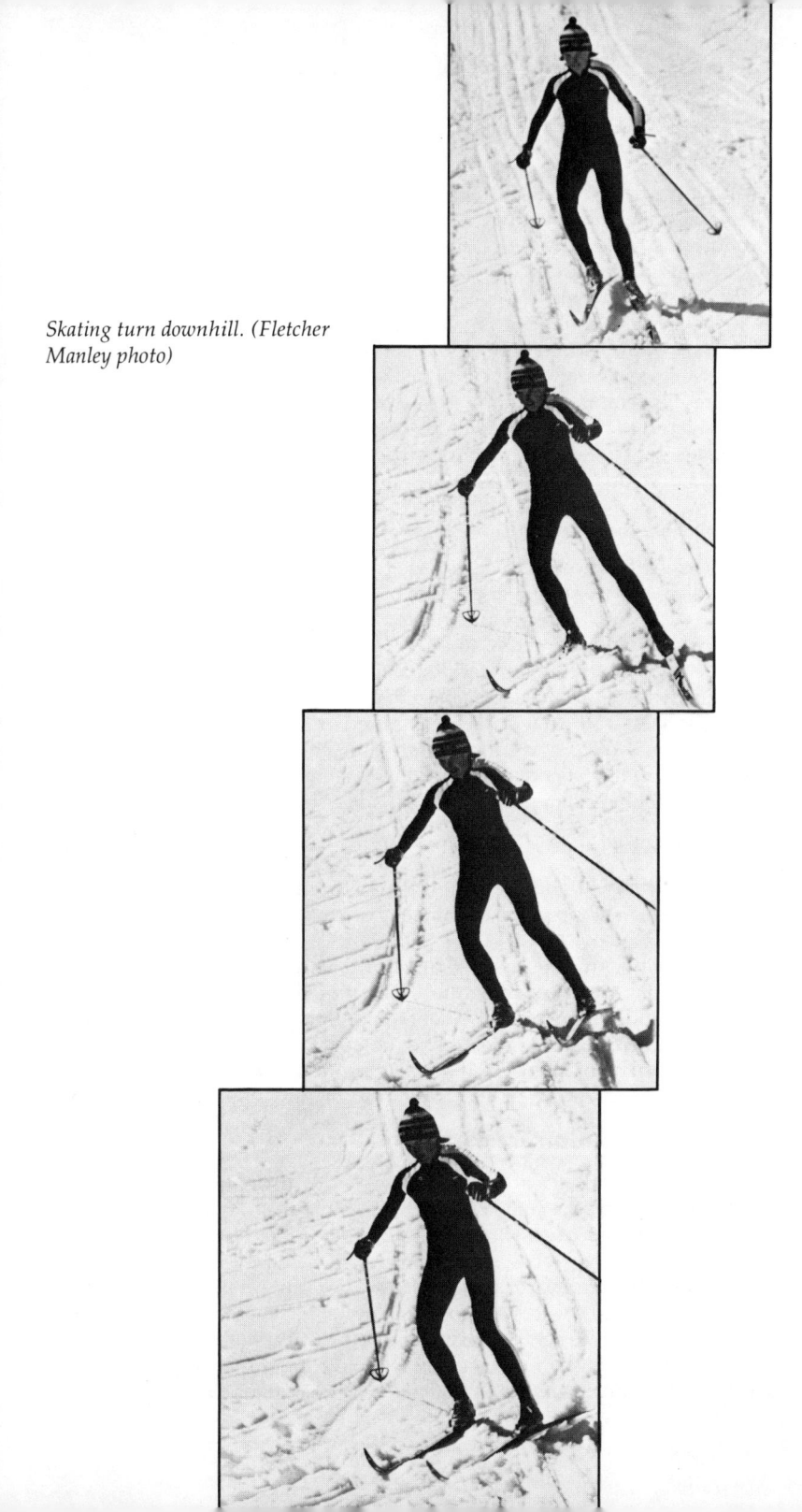

Glazed Tracks

Glazed tracks are those wobbly, underski snakes that occur most often when tracks are set in new, wet snow just at freezing, especially when the air humidity is high. A few skiers, sometimes no more than half a dozen or so, ski the track and presto! The glazed snakes appear.

There's only one way to ski under these circumstances: gently. Wax for a good kick or you won't have any kick. But as you ski the course, stay in the track. Get out of it and your good kick wax job will instantly become a magnet for every snow particle under your skis. Gentle skiing in glazed tracks requires more of an erect stance, and a lot more pole work than you normally use. Those who ski a lot of glazed tracks either complain of backaches or develop strong backs, because the combination of a more vertical stance and vigorous poling strains the back considerably.

Icy Tracks

Icy tracks differ from glazed tracks in that they usually occur at temperatures well below freezing, generally in older snow. Successive thawing and freezing of a snow cover reduces snow crystals to corn snow, and, with pressure such as in ski tracks, to ice.

Unlike glazed tracks, icy tracks usually are not wobbly. They are just horrifyingly fast; you would be amazed at the speed you can have in an icy track. The sides of the track may also be hard or icy, and jarringly unkind to your balance. You'll probably find yourself tensing up to maintain balance as you ski. The simplest cure is to slow down, keep your glide in control, and do a lot of double-poling.

Sloppy Tracks

If the snow is old and the temperature is well above freezing, you can almost count on sloppy tracks that feel like you're racing through mashed potatoes.

Such mush seldom poses any threat to balance or technique. It's just difficult to plug along, pushing the stuff out of your way. For these conditions, use a shorter stride and higher tempo. If the underlying snow base is firm, you can kick hard. In most cases, however, you will probably have to literally jog on your skis. Good arm-leg coordination is your best friend under these conditions.

Extremely Cold, Soft Tracks

A heavy snowfall at temperatures well below freezing, −15°C (5°F) or below, and fresh tracks in the new snow produce one of the most deceptive of track conditions. The tracks, especially if they were set by a track-setting vehicle, look as if they were cast in concrete. They may even feel that way for the first few hundred yards or so. But beware: stomp down and the track will give way. Send several skiers over an uphill section of the track and you get bumps, which are about as easy to ski as the washboard on a country dirt road is to drive. On these tracks you will have no problem waxing for ski grip; almost any cold snow wax will do. Your waxing problem will be in the

Skating turn — to intersecting track on the flat. (Fletcher Manley photo)

glide; do the best you can. With fast skis, you'll want to double-pole more. But be prepared to herringbone more hills because uphill tracks in powder are probably the most rapidly demolished of all tracks. If you are usually a Samson at poling, pretend that someone just cut your hair.

Slow Snow

Some snows, such as extremely fine, windblown snow and cold, fine-grained corn snow, are just plain slow to ski. If there's no wind and it's quiet, you can sometimes hear your skis grinding over the snow particles as if you were skiing on sand.

Here the technique is to find a comfortable forward speed and do everything possible to maintain it evenly. Don't hang onto your glide too long, or you'll lose forward momentum. Concentrate on a lot of diagonal striding at a high tempo. Reserve double-poling for downhills.

Some Transition Tricks

Snow conditions may differ along a course and change during a day or even during the race. Skiers in some citizens' races know that they may encounter three seasons in one race. The trick is to be alert. Always read the track ahead.

For most races, tracks are usually set no more than a few days in advance, and often on the morning of the race. So the in-track changes in snow conditions are most frequently caused by sun heating the snow. In midwinter, stretches of track in the sun are usually faster because they are slightly wetter. Shady areas of the track are colder, dryer, and slower. In the spring, or in areas that are farther south where the sun is higher in the sky, the opposite may be the case. The shady areas of the course are faster, while the slush in the sun is slower. This combination can go to extremes if the course winds through evergreen woods. During the day, the sun melts snow on the tree branches, and during the night, the meltwater on the track freezes to ice. The combination of ice in the shade and slush in the sun is a regular springtime curse.

In going from slow to fast snow, lean forward, or your skis may scoot out from under you. In going from fast to slow snow, lean back so you don't get tossed onto your nose.

The fast-to-slow transition is probably the one you'll have to handle most often in racing. If you need to get out of the track to ski around a fallen skier, you will probably ski into softer snow. If you get out of control on a downhill, you may want to step out onto untracked snow alongside the track to slow down. Any track set in windblown snow is always faster than the untracked snow around, even that between the two individual tracks. Lift out one ski and see how it slows you on this type of snow.

Icing and What You Can Do About It

Whenever you misjudge snow conditions and wax "too soft" (or "too warm"), you risk icing. Klister-wax is great for its intended snows, but without a doubt it is the number one icer if put on too thick or used in colder snow. Sometimes when snow and air temperatures are just at freezing, skis will ice up no matter what you do. In any case, icing is not a hopeless situation. You can combat it in several ways.

First and most obvious is to avoid icing if you can. When you are skiing courses where alternating sun and shade may cause icing, pick the happy medium in waxing and opt for a lessened overall performance rather than a great glide on wet snow and a dead stop on the dry stuff. Sometimes you may be skiing merrily along in an apparently excellent, unvarying track and suddenly you will ice up. You've fallen prey to the temperature sandwich effect, of which there are two types. The first type is most common in the Rockies and on the West Coast. The snow may be cold powder and the sun may blaze down from a cloudless sky, heating the upper snow layers to above freezing. If you wax well for this upper layer snow, and kick just a bit too hard or ski into an area shaded by a cloud, you have instant icing as your warm skis hit the cold snow. The second type is a temperature inversion, more common in the eastern U.S. and Canada where tracks often cross frozen lakes or streams. The ice on top of the water is insulated by a snow cover and may be partially melted, even though the air temperature may be considerably below freezing. Pressure from the water on the ice, shifting of the ice, and temperature cycling can all force water up on top of the ice. If you run into this overflow water while skiing through cold snow, you will have instant icing. The best cure in these situations is to double-pole through the troublesome section, keeping both skis well in contact with the snow. In doing so, you minimize underski pressure, and your skis will sink in less and cause less icing. If you've picked up overflow water or ski from dry into wet snow, wipe your skis well by gliding. If you happen to be diagonal striding at the time, cut down to a shuffle, keeping your skis on the snow because a ski kicked up in back contacts the colder air.

Once iced up, there's not much to do but scrape. For relatively minor icing of, say, just your grip wax, you probably can cross your skis and scrape one against the upturned edge of the other. Skiing across the upturned edges of another person's skis can be used in racing if you're skiing with a friend or have one among the spectators. The last resort is a full stop. Remove your skis, take out your scraper that you brought along in fear of this happening, and scrape away.

THAT NEW TECHNIQUE

The year 1974 is held to be a critical one for cross-country ski technique. Prior to that time, all cross-country skiers used what is now regarded as an old-fashioned technique, because of their heavy, slow, wooden skis. After that year, skiers switched to the *new technique*, made possible by the newer, lighter, faster fiberglass skis.

It's a wonderful story, but it simply isn't true. Developments in skiing, as in other sports, occur slowly, but steadily. What usually happens is that the best athletes evolve improvements and alterations in technique. They win. Others copy. It spreads.

The harbingers of the *new* cross-country technique were a handful of top international racers of the late 1960s and early 1970s. Foremost among them

(Top, left) *Odd Martinsen, 1970 World Ski Championships. (Michael Brady photo)*

(Top, right) *Otto Wiersholm, a decade plus after Martinsen. (Fletcher Manley photo)*

(Bottom) *Ole Ellefsaeter, 1968 Winter Olympic 50 km. (Michael Brady photo)*

was Norwegian Odd Martinsen, one of the first of the truly new breed of racer, a kid who had grown up racing. Formerly, racers were farm boys who had grown up skiing for utilitarian reasons, such as commuting to school and to and from farm chores. Martinsen just raced. He stood erect, with his weight more over his forward ski, than did his contemporaries. Other racers and coaches couldn't figure it out: he didn't ski "right," but boy, he surely did win, especially relay laps, where he was virtually unbeatable on the international circuit for six years. So racers started taking a closer look at what Martinsen did, and started doing it themselves. Martinsen's technique, if it can be be called that, was simple, neutral, and unidirectional—down the track, the way he was headed. Gone in his style were the exaggerated arm swings, upper body bobs, and rump dances then in vogue. He was simply a super efficient racer.

Martinsen was no one-man revolution. Before him, Swede Sixten Jernberg had run hills with a technique essentially identical to that now used by the top Russian racers, the current uphill masters. Finn Eero Mäntyranta had a double-pole that had to be seen to be believed. He had a style he perfected in the early 1960s on roller skis, to mention something else that isn't exactly new.

As for skis themselves, the *new* fiberglass racing skis are not necessarily all that new, or that much lighter, or that much faster than their wooden predecessors. Fiberglass skis were first used in major international meets in the 1968 Winter Olympics in Autrans, France, and again in the 1970 Nordic World Ski Championships in Vysoké Tatry, Czechoslovakia. Little was heard of these "breakthroughs," because the racers who used these skis did not win medals. That was to happen yet four years later, at the 1974 Nordic World Ski Championships in Falun, Sweden. Top Finnish, Swedish, and Norwegian cross-country wood racing skis of the late 1960s weighed 1,150 to 1,300 gr (2 lb, 8 oz to 2 lb, 14 oz) per 210-cm pair, equal to and in many cases less than the fiberglass and carbon-fiber racing skis of today. And given the right conditions, ski speeds of the 1960s were astounding: Harold Grönningen's record 14.4-mph average speed in a 10-km race in 1963 still stands,* and Ole Ellefsaeter's time in the 1968 Winter Olympic 50 km wasn't bettered until 1980, and then only by a little over one minute, out of a two-and-a-half hour event.

This is not to say that today's skiers aren't faster than their predecessors. They are. But they are for several reasons, not simply because they use fiberglass skis. First and foremost, today's racers are more scientifically trained and better conditioned athletes than those of decades past. Cross-country race courses and tracks are better than ever before, thanks to modern mechanized trail grooming and track setting. The 1966 and 1982 FIS Nordic World Ski Championships were both held in Oslo, in the same forest tract and along many of the same trails. In comparing the courses, the officials that supervised and the crews that set them, both remarked that the 1966 courses wouldn't even have met the minimum requirements for the 1982 courses, so much had the sport advanced.

---

*American Bill Koch has skied faster, but not in a race.

Competition is also keener, and more racers are racing at more levels than ever before. Depth in a sport always results in improvements in technique, as racers, teams, and nations compete for top placings. Finally, equipment is better. Skis are stronger and now rarely break in races. Poles are lighter, clothing is better-fitting and lighter, and boots and bindings are lighter and more flexible. These improvements in gear contribute to, but are by no means responsible for, the overall alterations in technique of the past decade.

Then how did the myth of the *new fiberglass technique* get started? It was probably due to the rebirth of cross-country skiing in North America. On the upswing since the early 1970s, the big wave of cross-country popularity swept over the U.S. and Canada in the mid-1970s. Before that time, only a handful of North Americans ever saw current top-level cross-country skiing: they were the ski teams sent abroad, usually only once a year, if that frequently. While the sport had slept for many decades in North America, it had gone forward abroad, and only a few North Americans knew what had taken place. The popularity of the sport in North America made more money available to send teams abroad, just as money became available to invite top European skiers to race on the North American continent. Suddenly, more Americans were exposed to top-level skiing than ever before, and it came as somewhat of a shock for most. And it happened just as fiberglass skis came on the market in quantity. So the two events were erroneously linked by many, who failed to realize that what they observed was not a new fiberglass technique, but simply a mad scramble to catch up.

6
WAXING

We have touted the pleasures of cross-country skiing in the past and have occasionally told the tour skier he could overlook written material on certain aspects of the sport if he was primarily interested in just getting out to have some fun. You may hear similar advice on waxing, coming from the waxless ski crowd. While this chapter is not a treatise debating the waxless versus waxable ski issue, we feel it is important to make a few points concerning waxless skis and lay them to rest.

Waxless skis play an important part in the scheme of things. They are convenient and have helped thousands of people get started easily. They will continue to be an important force in the market, and they will continue to improve. But, at this writing, they do not perform as well as waxable skis in most conditions.

You will hear about an occasional racer doing well on waxless skis. There are two notable examples. In 1976 Bill Koch skied a very fast section of the Olympic Relay, and in 1979 Per Knut Aaland finished second in the Holmenkollen 50 km. Both races were run under difficult snow conditions—new or fairly new snow at 0°C (32°F), packing to slithering tracks. But more important, both skiers were very strong, and on those days they made a good choice of skis. We never hear about the racers who chose waxless skis and failed to do well.

Some of the better waxless skis actually require waxing. The grip part of the ski base sometimes runs the length of the ski, or at least longer than most skiers need. So to improve the ski's performance, it is necessary to wax over the waxless base. Other waxless skis work best in particular conditions, and the manufacturers recommend waxing over the entire base in other conditions.

Since the combination of different skiers and different skis will always require different grip or kicker sections on the ski bases, a knowledge of waxing, or waxing theory, at a minimum, is necessary for the racer.

LEARN YOURSELF

How many times do racers make last-minute wax changes after learning that so-and-so is using a different wax? How many times do skiers go out to practice and wax according to what someone else has prescribed? In too many of these instances, the last-minute waxer or the copier finds the wax doesn't work—usually for some of the reasons mentioned below.

The practiced waxer can usually look at the snow and apply wax that will work. No hocus-pocus or incantation is necessary. He uses knowledge gained from past experience and a little information on the weather.

The experienced waxer is never thrown off by information that someone else is using a different wax. The veteran asks himself one question about his wax: "Does it work?" If the answer is "yes," it really doesn't matter who is using what, does it?

Some days you will have to be satisfied with a *ball-park wax*, which we define as one that slips some of the time, grabs or is slow part of the time, and runs well most of the time. That's the way it is some days. If you can accept it, you will be way ahead of the game. We've seen skiers spend hours looking for that perfect wax—which does not really exist for certain conditions—and never actually get down to the business of skiing.

If you are tempted to search for the perfect wax, think of car tires. The fanciest of imported radials can't be guaranteed to work perfectly all the time, even if you drive on only flawlessly asphalted interstates. Change the road surface slightly, for example, and you've got problems. Drive on dusty, filmy asphalt just after a rain and your tires won't grip.

At some races the organizers will prescribe a wax. The recommendation is usually worth trying, but once again, if you have knowledge and confidence in your own ability, stay with your own choice of wax.

NO CHARTS

Chances are you already have your own favorite wax brand or brands. In any event, no chart could ever be current for all waxes used in racing. So we

Several companies provide complete wax lines. (Fletcher Manley photo)

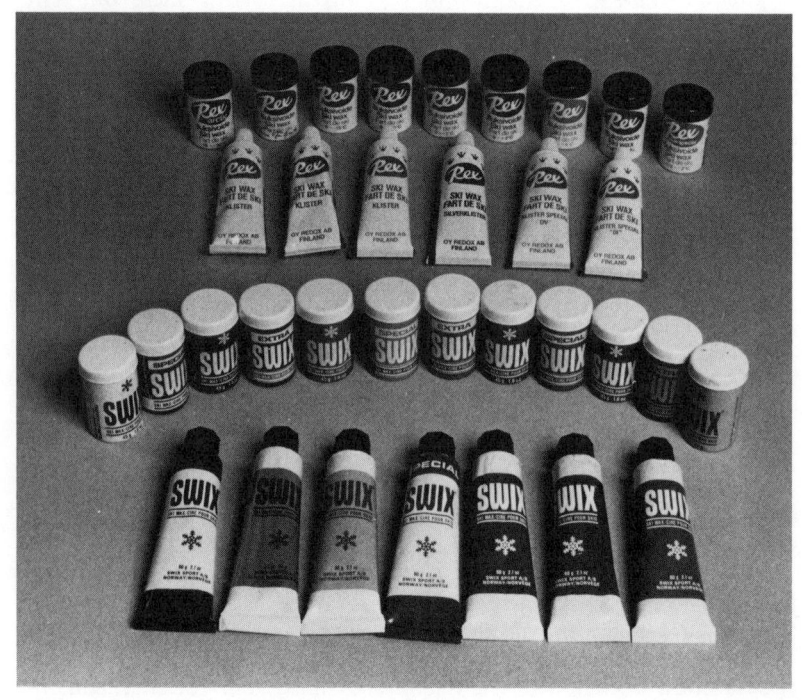

simply advise that you follow the manufacturer's directions for their spectrum of products.

All cross-country waxes and most glide waxes are now color coded in a rearranged version of the visible light spectrum. (Sandwiched between ultraviolet and infrared, the visible light spectrum is ordered as follows: violet, blue, green, yellow, orange, and red.) The waxes range from Green for harder waxes for colder snows through Yellow for the softer waxes for warmer snows. For instance, one company now offers a line of a dozen hard cross-country waxes. In order of the hardest through the softest they are: Polar, Green Special, Green, Green Extra, Blue Special, Blue, Blue Extra, Violet, Red Special, Red, Red Extra. Yellow. Remembering that order, and the general rule of *softer wax on wetter, warmer snow,* is an aid that we've found useful in wax selection.

NO WOOD HERE

Wood skis with wood bases are still around, but they are an endangered species, and in racing they are extinct. That's why in this book, which is about a form of racing, everything we say about waxing applies to fiberglass, carbon fiber, and other exotic-fiber-structure skis with thermoplastic bases.

NEW SKIS

Most new skis come out of the factory ready to be waxed. Some companies even melt a little glide wax on the tips and tails to help condition the ski base and get you started.

If the ski has not been waxed, we recommend cleaning it with a wax remover and lightly sanding it before waxing.

THE KICKER OR GRIP ZONE

The base of every pair of skis has, in the middle, a section of a certain length that is best suited for waxing with grip, purchase, or kicker wax. It's very important that you determine the length of this kicker or grip zone. It varies with different skiers, so you must experiment by waxing one ski slightly farther along than the other, then make comparisons between the skis to see which one works better.

In general, the kicker section extends from a point under the heel to a point a foot or so ahead of the toe. To find this section, squeeze the skis together and mark on the side walls the ends of the midsection that stays open until you put extreme pressure on the skis. Or use the paper test: Stand on both skis on a level surface and slide a piece of paper or an index card forward and back under the skis until it won't slide any farther. The boundaries mark a good approximation of your kicker zone.

The analytical person will note some drawbacks to this system. Two skiers could get the same results from the paper test by virtue of weighing the same. However, the stronger person would not need such a long kicker zone as the other.

As you experiment, you will find other variations, or will gain personal

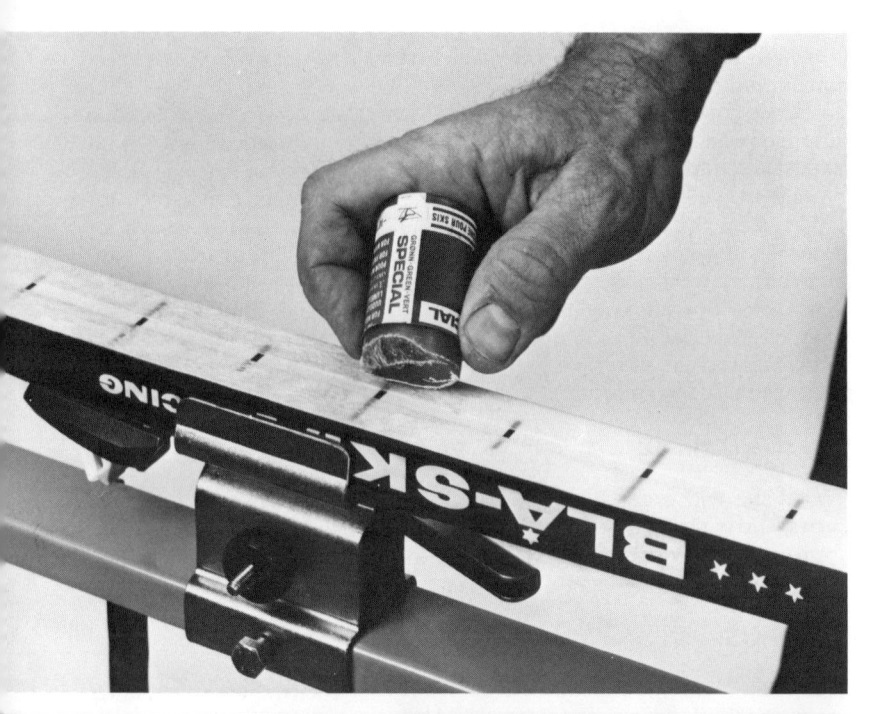

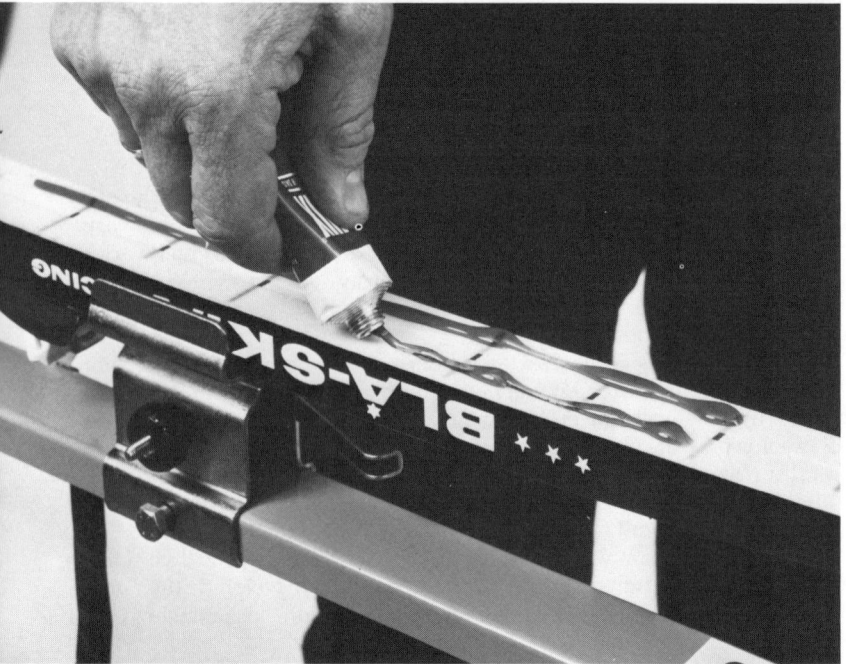

Apply hard wax or klister only in the center grip zone. (Frits Solvang photo)

preferences. Some top skiers, for example, start their kicker zone well behind the heel in certain powder conditions and shorten it in klister snow.

We emphasize that you must be the judge. Don't accept any firm standards.

THE GLIDE ZONE

The rest of the ski bottom that is not waxed for kicker will be waxed for glide—in most conditions. There are exceptions. The most notable is very cold, powder snow. As a minimum, most racers and coaches use a kicker wax, such as Green Special, or an even colder hard wax, from the heel to the tip. Sometimes they wax the entire length of the ski with this grip wax.

WAX SELECTION

Many old-timers will tell you that in the days before fiberglass skis, waxing was simpler because all they used was kicker wax over the entire length of the ski. No need then to choose a kicker wax *and* a glide wax! There's some truth to this, but even then most racers used a version of kick and glide wax when they put faster kick wax on tips and tails.

With fiberglass skis and the prevalent use of glide waxes, waxing is quicker than it used to be. Glide wax is easier to apply and easier to select than kicker wax. Also, if you ever have to rewax while training or racing, you'll appreciate fiberglass skis. In the days of wooden racing skis, rewaxing was a terror because wood absorbs water from snow. It was almost impossible to get wax to stick to wet ski bases. The thermoplastic bases on fiberglass skis are hydrophobic. One or two swipes with a dry cloth on these bases, and you can rewax with little or no difficulty.

The most important point in selecting wax is this: *Kicker wax is far more important than glide wax.* Don't spend large amounts of time agonizing over a choice of glide wax. Many racers and coaches put a broad-ranged glide wax on their skis the night before a race and let it go. The speed of your skis is primarily dependent on the length and selection of your kicker wax, not on the selection of a glide wax. After all, bare skis without glide wax aren't the slowest things going. In fact, some skiers slow their skis by selecting the wrong glide wax. We've also seen some top skiers and coaches spend so much time choosing glide wax that they have little time left for testing, choosing, and applying kicker wax.

The general waxing procedure is this: Determine the proper length for your kicker zone in all snow conditions, then learn to choose and apply kicker waxes. After all this—and it may take a long time to learn—you can begin to get fussy about glide wax.

Kickers: The Two-Wax System

If you want to simplify the selection of waxes, begin with a two-wax system. Several companies have two broad-ranged waxes, one for snow under 0°C (32°F) and one for snow above 0°C. These waxes do a good job and most expert waxers use them on occasions when it's difficult to fine-tune the wax selection.

Kickers: The One-Brand System

After you have learned the two-wax system, you can branch out and test all the waxes from one company's stockpile. This time-honored system works. Don't get impatient with your company's Blue, for instance. Adjust it by mixing something softer or harder with it—whatever seems to be warranted.

After That

If you go to a race and see someone open his wax kit to expose about a hundred different tubes of wax, you will know that one of the following situations exists:
1. He is trying to make an impression.
2. He uses the shotgun approach to waxing, trying a lot of different waxes in the hope that something will work.
3. He was told to buy a lot of different waxes.
4. He doesn't know what he is doing.
5. He perhaps does know something about all these waxes.

In any event, don't get psyched by appearances. When the time comes that you want to expand your one-brand wax kit, begin slowly. Test another company's Blue against your own. If you find it inferior, give it to someone who might be able to use it. If it is superior, replace your original Blue with the new one. If the new Blue complements the old Blue, keep them both and remember when they work.

Continue in this manner. We have our own favorites and stick with them because we like them and know their characteristics. It simply isn't necessary to try three different Blue waxes on a given day if you know the characteristics of your Blue. You can make any adjustments by knowing the characteristics of the next colder and the next warmer wax.

Hard Wax Versus Klister

Many skiers still get confused over when to use klisters and hard waxes. Here are a few clues:

Use hard wax on almost all new snow, unless the temperature is around 0°C (32°F) and the track is glazed. Then a light layer of Yellow or Orange klister might work, especially if you cover it with some soft hard wax. Klister-waxes, which are combinations of hard and klister waxes, are designed for just those conditions. Most wax makers list them as hard waxes because they come in the same tins as hard waxes.

Use klisters if the snow has melted and refrozen to hard granular snow or melted again to wet corn snow.

If the snow is old and has been skied on a lot, or well worked over by snow-packing machinery, some klisters can be particularly effective. This is especially true of klisters of the Blue, Purple, and Silver range. Or klisters may be used in a thin coat as binders for some hard wax.

When you don't know whether to use hard wax or klisters, think of the snow categories for which each was made. If the snow is definitely new—you can see it falling or see that it still looks new—then hard waxes are your best

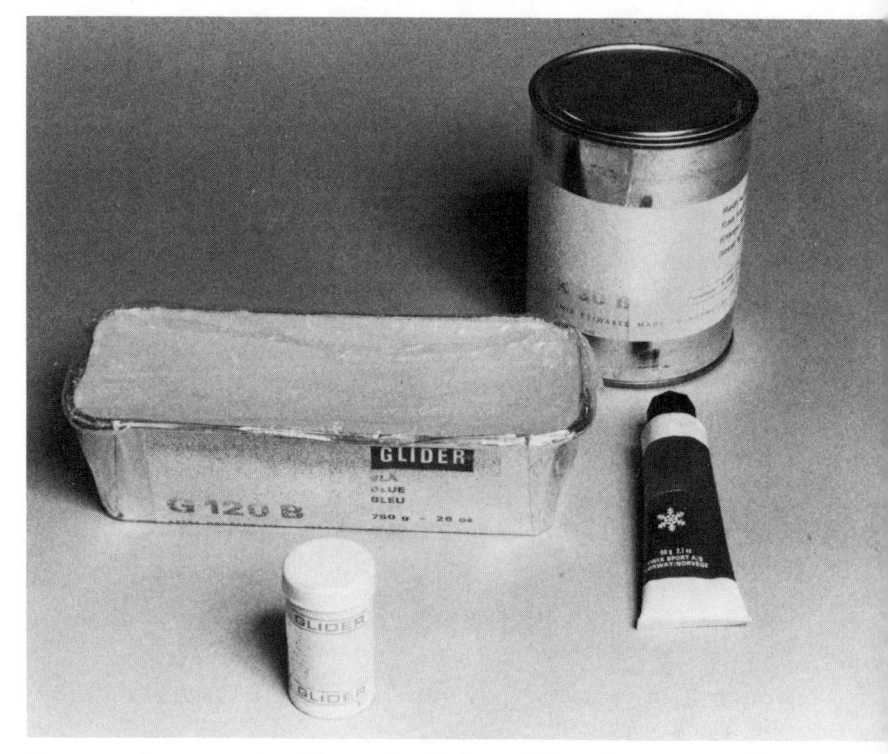

If you wax for a team, you will appreciate the larger bulk packages, compared here with the common individual-sized packages. (Fletcher Manley photo)

bet. But if you know that the snow has been altered—by successive thaw-freeze cycles, rain, or absorbed sunshine—then klisters are probably best.

Glide Wax

You can make out famously for a long time with three kinds of glide wax: one for warm conditions, one for colder snow, and a cross-country hard wax for the very coldest of conditions. We recommend cross-country glide waxes instead of alpine waxes, because cross-country waxes are designed to last longer at the higher underski pressures and lower ski speeds of cross-country.

Glide waxes can be combined. If you feel your warm weather glide wax is a bit soft for the present conditions, mix in some cold snow wax. If cold snow wax seems to have a lot of moisture in it, mix in some soft snow glide wax. And so on. (See "All Those Variables" later in this chapter.)

After you have learned to hit the kicker wax every time and know how to use your glide waxes, then you can branch out and test more glide waxes. But don't go off the deep end. Be selective. Don't permit yourself to get to that self-doubting stage, when you really have too many waxes to test or haven't used some of the ones in your kit in such a long time that you have forgotten how they work. If this happens, you are back to square one.

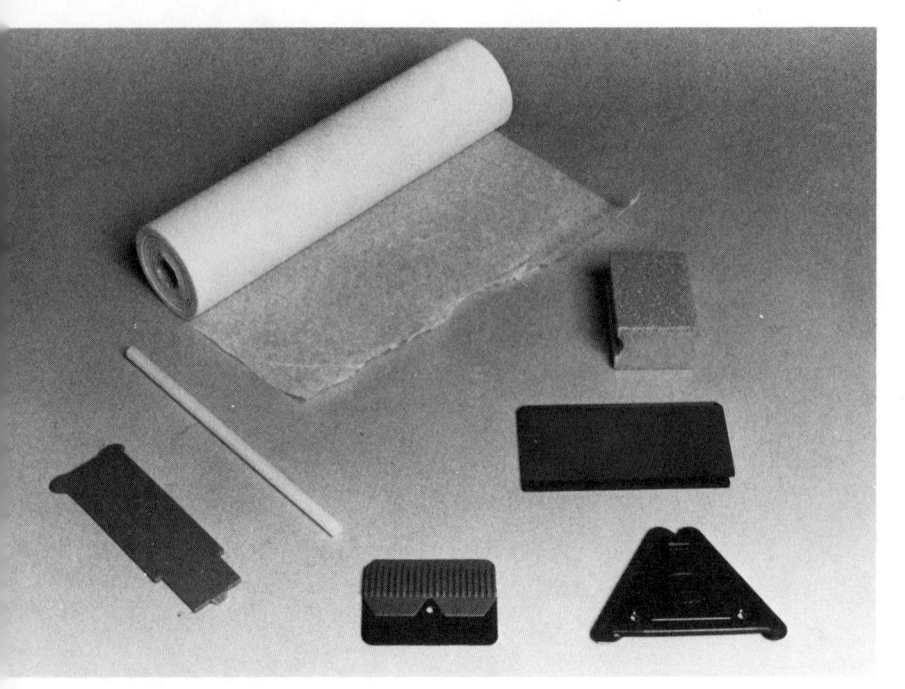

A variety of scrapers, wiping tissue, corks, and a base repair candle should be in every wax kit. (Fletcher Manley photo)

Polished Glide Wax

Let's say you've picked just the right glide wax and have applied it beautifully for cold snow: the mirror-polished tips and tails of your skis give you a rocket glide in the track. You go to bed pleased with your test waxing. But then overnight, it warms up; the snow on race day is almost wet. "Wow!" you think. "Now I'll outglide them all!" If you were that good on cold snow, you should be far better on warmer snow where glide is easier. Right?

Wrong! You're better off doing a quick rewaxing for glide. Here's why. In running a cold glide wax on warm snow, all you've done is reversed the roles of wax and snow. When the glide wax is too soft for the snow involved, the harder snow particles dig into the wax and slow your glide. But the opposite also holds: when the glide wax is too hard for the underlying wet snow, the harder wax surface digs into the softer snow and also slows your glide. In such mismatches, snow can dig into wax or wax can dig into snow. The glide waxing ideal is to match wax hardness to snow hardness, so neither gives way to the other.

Suction can also brake glide when you use glide wax that is too hard for wet snow. You know the effect if you've ever tried to pick up a small mechanical part, such as a smooth-surfaced nut, from the bottom of an oily pan. You chase the nut all over, trying to get hold of it. The same thing happens when a water film from wet snow spreads out over a smoothly polished glide wax surface. Your skis suck onto the snow. You can break that suction by waxing with a softer glide wax and/or by striating the glide wax—putting lengthwise scratches in its surface along the base. The scratches give the snow-water film a place to flow, which breaks suction.

When Not to Glide Wax

Skis glide best at −4°C (25°F). Below this temperature, glide decreases until, at about −70°C (−99°F), snow is just like sand, as far as glide is concerned. This is why waxing for glide at low temperatures is always a tricky business and why there are so many ways to do the job. At temperatures of −12°C (10°F) and below, hard cross-country waxes glide as well as most glide waxes. So one approach is to wax the entire ski base with a harder cross-country wax, spreading the grip out, so to speak, rather than striving for good glide on tips and tails and applying a kicker wax for grip. In other words, when it's really cold, use cross-country wax all the way. Swedish racer Thomas Wassberg did just that for the 1980 Lake Placid Olympic 15 km, which was run in temperatures of −12° to −15°C (5° to 10°F) and air humidity of 90 percent. Wassberg waxed his entire ski bases with a hard wax and won the race.

APPLICATION

The most overlooked and underestimated part of waxing is application. We have seen too many skiers slap some wax on only to find that it doesn't work. Then they slap something else on that doesn't work either, and give up. If only they had properly applied the first coat, they might have enjoyed their skiing.

Take care when waxing. Begin with a warm, dry ski and apply the wax carefully, smoothing it so it is free of bumps, ridges, and globs.

There are many different methods of applying wax, but we've found that the best overall method is also the easiest. Apply the wax and use heat to smooth it. There are variations on this theme, which we will explain, but in general you will be well off if you follow this practice.

Preferably Warm, Always Dry

It's always easier and most often more comfortable to wax indoors than out. Warm skis make both the application and the bonding of wax easier than cold skis.

The one virtually inflexible rule for waxing skis is: *Dry the skis first*. Wax simply doesn't adhere to water. Even if you are successful in waxing a pair of partially wet skis, the moisture trapped under the wax will freeze when you ski out on the track, and the wax will flake off. So whenever you wax indoors, stay away from showers or other wet places where there is moisture that can condense on your skis. Carry a couple of cloths in your wax kit to wipe skis dry before you wax. Terry cloth is a good bet for clean skis or skis waxed with the hardest of hard waxes, but a horror if you have to dry a pair of skis waxed with klister. A lint-free rag is best for those jobs but takes longer because it doesn't absorb so much moisture.

How Long, How Thick?

Most people can read the wax tin labels and make a good selection, but getting the right length and thickness of application is the key. In general, the longer the kicker, or the thicker the coat, the more grip you get. Conversely, a short kicker, or a thin coat, does not provide so much grip but is slightly faster.

As mentioned earlier, most skiers mark the kicker zone on their skis and use this as a guide for putting on kicker wax. However, there may be times when you will have to vary the length or thickness, depending on such factors as the track conditions, the snow conditions, and the temperature and humidity.

Hard Wax Application

Rub hard wax on a clean, dry ski in a warm room and then iron it to smooth it out. Set the skis outside to cool. Heat changes a wax's characteristics and makes it a bit faster and more slippery, so if your wax selection is already a borderline case—using Green, for instance, on a day that may call for Blue—it's a good time to put on an extra coat outside. Adding this extra coat, which should be corked in, will give you more grip and let you know if your original wax has cooled enough.

Klister Application

Squeeze the klister on the running surface and then smooth it with the palm of your hand (our favorite method), or with the edge of one of those plastic paddles that come with some klisters, or with a straightedge. The klister should look glassy smooth when it has been spread. Set the skis outside to cool. There is no need to add extra klister for grip. If you have chosen the right klister you will have plenty of kick. The klister should be about as thick as a fresh coat of paint.

Instead of Wax

The latest racing waxing trick for troublesome new snow at temperatures slightly above freezing is to rough-sand the kicker zone of the ski base with #80 to #100 sandpaper to create a coarse surface that grips, and then spray silicone over the sanded area so it will slide. The method can do wonders when no kicker wax seems to work well. But it is hard on bases; a few such treatments and you'll go through a standard racing ski base. So unless you have plenty of skis, we don't recommend the trick.

Binder

There are three kinds of binder currently used by racers.

The most common is the one used for hard-wax conditions. This binder comes in a tin, just like other hard waxes, and you apply it like a hard wax, rubbing it on and smoothing it with an iron. Some binders rub on easier if the ski base is warmed with the iron first.

Sometimes a regular hard klister, such as Blue, is used in a thin coat as a binder for hard waxes or softer klisters. If you are using klister as a binder for

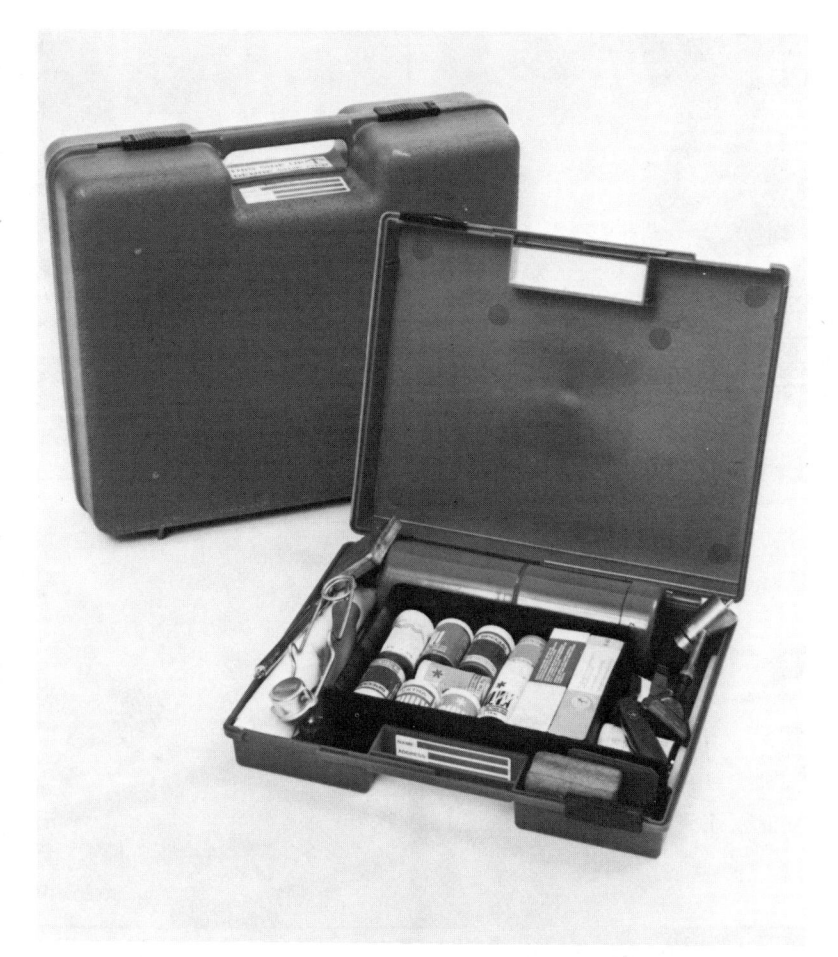

A small wax kit will hold all you ever really need to take to a race. A larger variety is useful if you wax for a team or want to carry a season's supply with you. (Frits Solvang photo)

hard wax, put on a thin coat and set the skis outside so that the klister can harden. The hard wax should be corked on over the top of the klister. Do it outside so that the klister does not get too soft and mix with the hard wax.

A fairly new method for helping to keep soft klisters, such as Reds and Yellows, from rolling off the running surface onto the side walls is first to apply a thin layer of Blue klister, let it set up, and then put the soft klister over it.

The third binder is Chola and it is used as a klister binder, especially for Blue or Purple klisters. With present day track-setting machinery, the snow is not so harsh as it used to be and we don't see Chola used so often. If conditions warrant the use of softer klisters, there is usually not a problem of

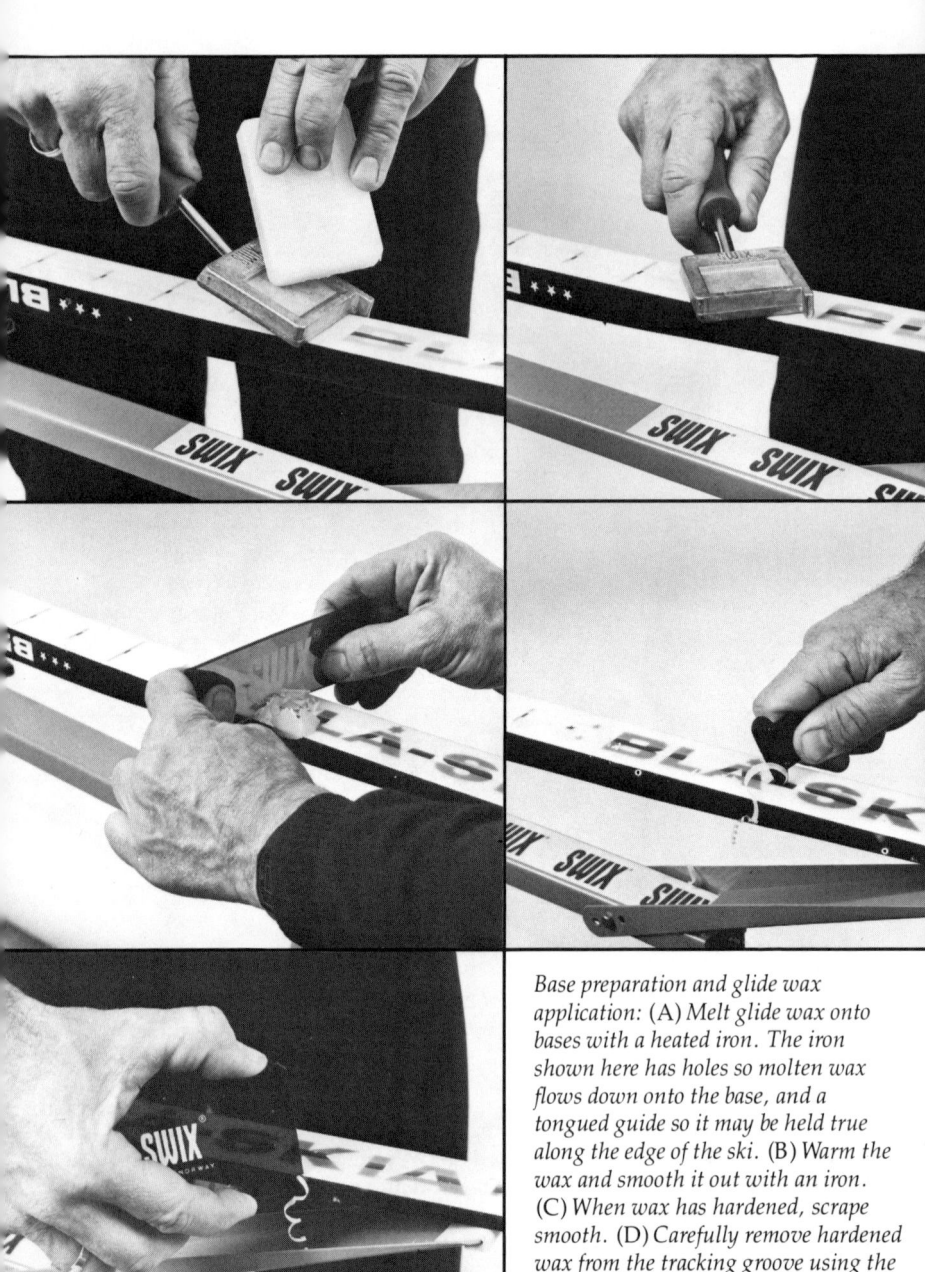

Base preparation and glide wax application: (A) Melt glide wax onto bases with a heated iron. The iron shown here has holes so molten wax flows down onto the base, and a tongued guide so it may be held true along the edge of the ski. (B) Warm the wax and smooth it out with an iron. (C) When wax has hardened, scrape smooth. (D) Carefully remove hardened wax from the tracking groove using the rounded end of a klister-spreader paddle. (E)Clean edges and remove wax dripped onto side walls using a notch in the scraper. (Frits Solvang photos)

wear, so Chola is not used much with Red, Yellow, or Orange klisters. However, some skiers have mixed Chola with hard wax for granular snow, which softens as more and more people ski over it.

Glide Wax Application

The method most often recommended for applying glide wax is to hold it against a hot iron and drip it onto the ski. Then iron the wax on, let it cool, and scrape off the excess wax. Most waxers agree that the finished job should be very thin and smooth for cold powder snow, and a bit thicker and perhaps not so smooth for warmer snow. For best glide in cold snow, buff the surface with a plastic scouring pad to remove all surface wax. For wet snow, put grooves in the wax job by using a wire brush and drawing it the length of the waxed area. This allows the water in the snow and the track a chance to escape, or to prevent it from building up suction on the ski bottom. Have you seen those tire ads with the water streaming through the little grooves in the tire? Same idea!

We have found that first rubbing the glide wax on the ski and then ironing it in is just as efficient as the more common method and is also more economical. In fact, we seldom have much wax to scrape off the ski after ironing.

You will hear different theories on glide wax, but our feeling remains the same: glide wax is not nearly so important as grip wax. Spend your extra time trying to fine-tune your grip or kicker wax job.

Choosing a Torch

The best torches for ski waxing and cleaning are the small, hand-held propane cylinder or butane cartridge types. You can buy them in hardware, outdoor supply, and ski shops. The simplest torch kits usually have all you need: a fuel cylinder/cartridge, a universal burner, a flame spreader, and a spark lighter.

Propane cylinders are heavier than butane cartridges with the same amount of liquified gas, but they light more easily and burn more steadily at subfreezing temperatures. If you carry your torch to races in a wax kit, the propane variety is probably your best bet. If you backpack a torch, you may want to trade convenience for light weight and opt for the butane variety.

If you fly to races and take your wax torch along, leave the gas containers behind. Both federal and international aviation safety regulations forbid their transport on aircraft. (This is why mail order houses always state that gas containers must be shipped via surface transportation.) For air travel in North America, use a propane cylinder torch, because refill cylinders are available in hardware stores throughout the U.S. and Canada. If you travel abroad on the World Loppet circuit, you're probably better off with one of the European-made butane torches. North American and European propane torch burners are similar, and some are even made by the same company. But the threads where the cylinders and burners mate differ: burners with North American threads won't fit European cylinders, and vice versa.

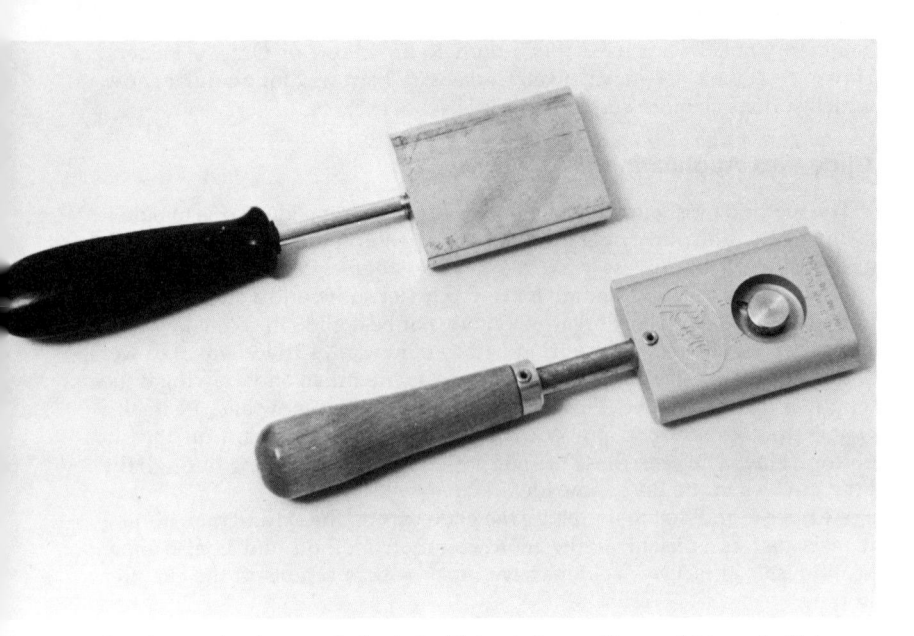

Popular waxing irons, to be heated with torch flames. One model has a built-in thermostat. (Frits Solvang photo)

Sanding for Improved Glide

One of the current rages in cross-country ski racing is sanding plastic ski bases to improve glide. It is a practice inherited from alpine ski racing and jumping, where competitors are concerned exclusively with glide. Although it has some advantages, we don't recommend it in most cases.

We've seen new skis so beautifully turned out from the factory that all you have to do is mount bindings and apply grip wax for superb racing. But we've also seen an unfortunately large number of new skis that obviously need base sanding to be skiable. The telltale defect is a hill-and-dale ripple along the base. Other common defects, often caused by poor quality control in laminating bases to skis, are railed (concave) and bowed (convex) bases. When you sand bases with any of these defects, you are not "fine-tuning" the skis for racing; you are finishing the factory's work. Our advice is not to buy a pair with such defects. Let the factory do its own finishing; they have machines for it.

We regard base sanding as either obviously useful, or conditionally marginal. There are only two reasons to sand: (1) new bases often need a light touch-up to remove nicks and oxide picked up in shipping and storage; and (2) old bases, roughened or otherwise damaged in use, frequently need truing or repair. Even in these obviously necessary cases, sanding is useful, not mandatory. We know carpenters and others skilled with their hands who do wonders with sharp refinishing scrapers, and never touch their ski bases with sandpaper.

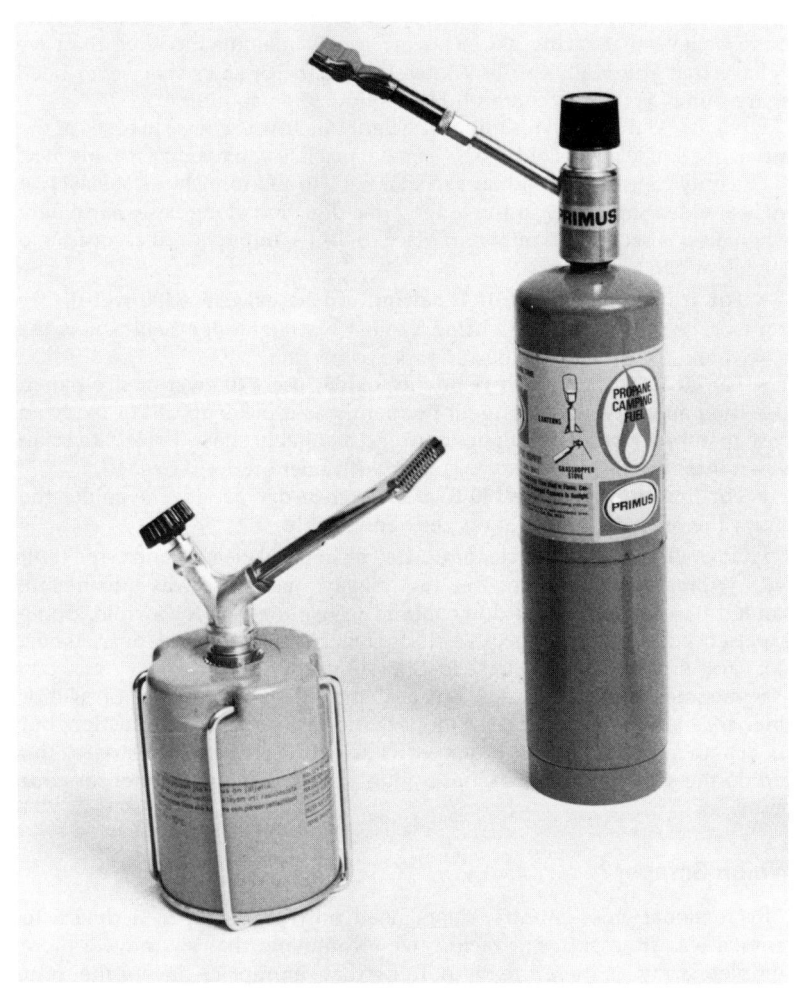

Butane cartridge torch and propane cylinder torch. (Frits Solvang photo)

In the conditionally marginal category are all sanding methods aimed to improve the glide of otherwise smooth, flat, undamaged, unoxidized ski bases. We have no doubts that a scientifically perfect match of ski glide zone properties to course tracks would involve some sanding. But we have yet to see a practical system for achieving such a match and, at best, regard it as a one-percent solution. For every touted triumph of the sanders, we know of dozens of unheralded triumphs of nonsanders, if that's the way to divide the practitioners. Aside from these matters, our major objection to sanding for performance is that it's both time-consuming and difficult to do properly. Even those skilled in the art often spend three or four hours sanding a single pair of ski bases.

We have to admit, however, that sanding sometimes is necessary. We no more believe that racing ski bases are totally maintenance-free than we believe that you really can buy knives, scissors, or saws that never need sharpening, as the ads contend. Here's how to go about it.

First, assess the job. If it's minor—a light touch-up of new ski bases or the repair of a single nick in old bases—treat it just like you would a waxing job.

Use only wet-or-dry sandpaper that is fixed to a sanding block at least two inches wide. Sand only in the lengthwise direction along bases, and only when a ski is securely clamped in place. Select sandpaper grit according to the job at hand:

- **For truing base flaws or repairing old bases, use #100 wet-or-dry paper.** Check flatness by sighting against a straightedge held across the base. Follow with finer grades of paper as needed.
- **For cleaning bases and removing oxide, use #100 wet-or-dry paper.** Use the paper dry, and change it frequently as it picks up dirt or oxidized base material. Wrap a bit of paper around a suitably shaped object to clean down into the tracking groove. Follow with finer grades if needed.
- **For fine-tuning, use #180 to #320 wet-or-dry paper.** The colder the snow, the finer the grade. Sand glide zones only.

Follow all sanding with cleaning. Use a chemical cleaner and wipe it off with wiping tissue or a lint-free rag. Always melt base wax into freshly sanded bases, even if you don't intend to use the skis for awhile. Some experienced skiers melt wax in a thick layer before they store or transport skis, and finish-scrape the base just before use.

Sometimes suction between skis and snow slows your glide on wet or fine, dry snow. Longitudinal striations in the base can break the suction, but there's no need to chew up bases with a wire brush in order to striate. You can do the same job after you have glide waxed; it is much better for your bases.

Which Scraper?

Recreational cross-country skiers need only one scraper, a device to remove wax from skis. For racing, we recommend that you have a more complete array, as there's really nothing that can replace having the right tool for the job at hand. There are two types, which we term *wax scrapers* and *ski scrapers*.

- **Wax scrapers.** These are used by all skiers to remove wax from skis. Made of different metals and plastics, they come in many shapes and sizes, and are often combined with other implements such as waxing corks, screwdrivers, or bottle openers. Their scraping blades are not necessarily flat or straight, because they are intended to scrape wax *up* off a base, much as a cook uses a spatula to scrape food out of a frying pan.
- **Ski scrapers.** These are for more serious work, such as scraping glide paraffin, truing bases, and removing surface oxide. They are usually rectangular, about three by five inches, and made of tool steel or hard plastic. We recommend the plastic variety for scraping wax, because plastic is easier on bases than steel should you slip when scraping and gouge the base. The

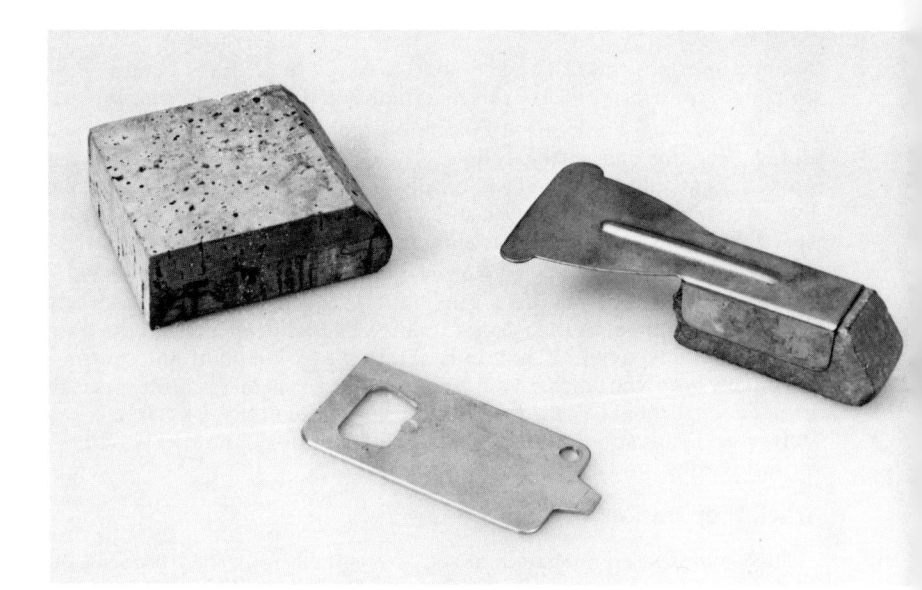

Scrapers and corks can be combined into a handy unit that fits in a pocket in a race. Some scrapers have other features, such as bottle openers and screwdrivers. (Frits Solvang photo)

steel variety is a must for scraping base plastic. A quality scraper will last a lifetime if it is regularly cleaned and sharpened.

Corks

Waxing corks, as their name implies, were once made of natural cork. But most of them are now synthetic, and we recommend that type because they seldom crumble and leave bits of cork in the wax, as did natural corks. In use, you may think that new corks do a better job than old ones. Not so. Look at the cork: a new cork just picks up more wax than an old one, fooling you into thinking you've done the job more quickly.

Just as you wouldn't intentionally apply the "wrong" wax, you shouldn't mix corks. Wax picked up by a cork can flake off later as you rub in another wax, contaminating its surface. So it's best to use at least four corks: one for binder, one for hard waxes, one for glide waxes, and one for tackier hard waxes, such as klister-wax. Label each one on its end with a felt-penned letter or symbol, such as B for binder, G for glide, H for cold snow hard wax, and K for klister-wax.

CONSIDERATIONS BEFORE WAXING

Before selecting a wax for yourself, you need to do some armchair waxing. The more thought you put into your waxing before actually beginning to test waxes, the better. Too often, skiers find some wax that works in the starting area or stadium, and neglect the most important factors.

Trail Profile

Good wax jobs run fast and climb well. However, there are times when you might want faster skis, or skis that climb better. Here are two examples:

- One of the 5-km loops at Putney, Vermont, has a long, quite rugged uphill near the end of the course. The 3-km section preceding this is predominantly downhill and technically demanding. Skiers gain time here by virtue of skiing ability, not fast wax jobs. So it doesn't pay to wax for speed. Smart skiers wax for the climb in this race.
- The Vasaloppet in Sweden is an example of the opposite extreme. From its start, the course climbs just 149 m (489 ft) in the first 3 km. It's essentially flat to the 20-km point, then drops almost steadily for 30 km. But the drop isn't much, only about 250 m (825 ft). From the 55-km point, the course is essentially flat to the finish. In the whole 85.6-km race, there are only 5 km of track on what could be called an uphill grade. Most of that 5 km is near the start, where you can't ski anyway because of the crowd. The Vasa is a course for fast waxing, and a lot of double-poling.

Track Preparation

The way tracks are prepared, or set, affects their properties. If tracks are packed by people on snowshoes or skis, followed by skiers skiing in the track, chances are that the in-track snow is pretty much like the surrounding snow. The same can be true of tracks set by smaller snowmobiles pulling track setters. But tracks set by heavier machines (now used for most major race courses) can differ considerably from the surrounding snow. The most extreme case is when tracks are set in old, hard, or crusty snow that is covered by a thin layer of powder (itself not deep enough to hold a track). The machines dig up the older, underlying snow, and chew it together with the newer powder. Even though every skiing experience may tell you that your favorite hard wax would be ideal for that powder, start with a binder. The older snow, especially in the broken pieces ground up by the machines, is about as kind to wax as sandpaper. You may even elect to use klister first (for the underlying old snow) topped with a cover layer of hard wax (for the powder), as you do for sandwich tracks.

Sandwich Tracks

Almost everything you read about waxing tells you to wax for the prevailing snow. Snow can vary, and tracks can change. That's one of the breaks of the game. But what if you have more than one type of snow at a time? For example, how do you wax for firm, hard tracks set the day before in old snow, which is dusted lightly during the night with a layer of new powder? Like a deli sandwich, you know that both the salami and the rye are there; each component of the sandwich stands out.

If you wax for the firm, old-snow tracks, you'll quickly ice up in the new powder. If you wax for the new powder, it had better be a short race, because you won't have much wax left after 5 to 10 km.

There are two ways of handling the sandwich situation. Both call for putting hard wax on top of soft, which is just what we tell recreational skiers not to do. It's a technique for advanced waxers only, and it usually won't hold for an entire day's skiing—but that's usually no concern when you're racing.

The first situation is when the hard base tracks call for a softer variety of hard wax, such as Blue Extra. Start with a good base binder wax job, then apply the Blue Extra as if the sandwich problem didn't exist. Apply two coats of wax, corking each one as smooth as you can. Then cool your skis by setting them outside for about half-an-hour. When they have cooled, bring them inside and cover the Blue Extra with softened wax for the powder. Soften the wax by passing the exposed wax in a can through a torch flame. Quickly rub it on and cork it out before it hardens again. (Some racers use their labeled corks for this purpose to avoid contaminating the wax job with wax from a "wrong" cork.) Then let the skis cool again before test skiing.

The second situation is when the base tracks call for a klister. Start by warming in a good kicker of klister, being meticulous about getting it smooth. Let the skis cool outside for about half-an-hour, then cover the klister with hard wax for the powder. Apply it in long, light strokes, exerting about as much pressure as you would use to draw long lines with chalk on a blackboard. Smooth out the hard wax with light corking. Beware of excess pressure, as you can easily dig into the softer, underlying klister. When you have finished, let the skis cool again before test skiing.

Changing Track Conditions

We've seen many racers and coaches wax for the moment before a race. Usually, the snow in the track is colder, harsher, or sharper at the beginning of a race. After several racers get in the tracks, the snow is ground down to a more mealy consistency. Loose snow gets piled into the track as well.

On the other hand, if you are the first person over a track or are starting very early in a race with few forerunners, your wax will probably get worn off quickly unless you have applied adequate binder. Snow crystals change overnight and a mealy track one evening can be like sandpaper the next morning.

So, your position in the field—whether it's an interval or a mass start—should be considered as you make a prediction regarding the condition of the snow in the track and wax accordingly.

Weather Forecast

Before waxing, you should know the weather forecast. Is it going to cool or get warmer? If there is to be a change in the cloud cover, how will it affect the snow?

We know a coach who once waxed for an eclipse of the sun. It was a wet, corn snow day and when the sun went under, the snow cooled rapidly. Our friend outwaxed the field that day.

Temperature Report

It's wise to take air and snow temperatures before waxing, especially before a race. If you are familiar with your own thermometers, don't bother with the race organizers' temperature report, unless you need it from a point on the course where you can't test yourself. Your thermometers might not jibe with the organizers', which could be crucial when waxing around 0°C (32°F).

Humidity and Moisture Content of Snow

Snow can measure −6°C (21°F) and be dry, requiring Green wax, or it can be −6°C and contain a lot of moisture and require Blue, or Blue Extra. Don't expect to use the same wax every time the snow temperature is the same.

All ski wax makers compound their products and label them for average winter humidities. Fog, mist, and high air humidity make snow wetter than it might otherwise be at the same temperature. This requires that you wax with a softer, or warmer, wax than indicated by the directions on the container. Conversely, for unusually dry conditions, such as in the Rocky Mountains, you may have to wax harder, or drier, than indicated by the wax manufacturer.

Air and Snow Temperatures

The directions on most wax containers are designed for air temperatures. This makes it easier for waxers, but there are instances where the air temperature can be misleading. We have already mentioned the importance of humidity and moisture content of snow. Air thermometers don't check this for you.

Also, it's important to know that snow temperatures are usually colder than air temperatures. In some cases, the snow can be several degrees cooler, such as during a warm day following several cold ones.

Snow temperatures change more slowly than air temperatures. Take this into account, especially after a cold day. The snow may permit the use of Green when the thermometer tells you it's time for Blue.

Falling Snow

When snow is falling, snow and air temperatures will be very close. If you

---

Check Out the Reports

At a big citizens' race in Switzerland, I was testing wax and checked out the temperature board to see what it indicated. To my amazement the organizers said the snow temperature at the start was 1.5°C (35°F). I hurried over to the officials to check on this phenomenon, and after several spurts of my poor German answered by some equally confusing Schweizerdeutsch, I determined that they were telling me there was water in the track. They had put the tip of the thermometer right on the surface, where the snow was very wet.

So, if you run into a temperature report like this one, don't rush for your water skis. Check it out first. —JC

have some temperature points (see the next section), you can get pretty close to the right wax by using just one thermometer.

Temperature Points

In powder snow conditions, it's helpful to have snow temperature points to use as references. For instance, when the snow rises in temperature to −5°C (23°F), it's a good time to use Blue Extra and Special waxes. Straight Blue might work in very dry conditions at this temperature, but be ready to switch.

If the snow is very cold, below −10°C (14°F), it's a good time to try Green Specials or colder snow waxes.

Variation in the Snow

There's snow and there's snow. Good waxers can look at and feel the snow and get a good idea of its qualities without consulting temperature reports. If you learn to do this, you will find that sharper or harsher snow calls for harder waxes, just as softer, more rounded snow crystals call for softer waxes.

There are a few other tip-offs used by expert waxers to "sense" the snow. Some of these "secrets" are strictly local—what the snow is like when it blows in from the south, what it's like when smoke from the power plant blows this way, and so on. But a few of the trade secrets are general:

The sun warms snow, making it wetter than surrounding snow not exposed to sunlight. For equivalent conditions of clear sky, the amount of

To test snow, grab a handful. (Michael Brady photo)

heat that snow absorbs from the sun depends on: the age of the snow (dirty snow absorbs more sunlight); the angle of the slope and the direction it faces (steep, southern exposures absorb the most in the Northern Hemisphere); the latitude (the farther south, the more intense the solar radiation); and the time of day and year (midday is always the warmest time and mid-December is the least sunny month). For a race in the sun, you should wax warmer than the air temperature indicates.

Altitude affects waxing, but only secondarily, at least at altitudes where ski races are held. More important are the other factors that go hand in hand with altitude: higher areas are usually less humid (colder wax); the snow may come from moisture evaporated from cleaner inland lakes rather than the sea (also colder wax); less cloud cover and less air pollution make the sun warmer (warmer wax); and nights may be colder (colder wax).

Artificial snow is often considerably different from natural snow. Though still somewhat of a stranger in cross-country, artificial snow is sometimes trucked in to patch up a course. So beware. Usually made from well water, it may look and act like natural snow, but the mineral impurities in the well water act like antifreeze, pushing the freezing point downward. This means that at temperatures a few degrees below freezing, artificial snow may start to melt. When in doubt, always test wax on artificial snow, starting with a wax job that's warmer than you might otherwise select.

Technique Changes

If in considering numerous factors, you miss the correct wax, then you'll have to adjust your technique accordingly. If your wax is too soft or slow, it is unwise to try for long gliding strides. Shorten your step so you don't tire so quickly. On the other hand, if your wax slips and is very fast, you will have to use all the double-poling possible.

ALL THOSE VARIABLES

Anytime two people try to do anything connected with waxing, you have a situation with variables. If you test wax with someone or for someone, or if someone tells you what is working for him, you have variables. It pays to know this.

Here is how some of the variables creep in.

Wax Selection

This one is obvious. You might be using one color wax and someone else is using another color. But your skis probably work differently. Or, you might be using one brand of Blue and someone else has another brand of Blue. Blues may behave differently.

There's another parameter in wax selection: Is the wax new or old? There are two ways of defining the situation.

First, is the wax new or old on your skis? For constant snow conditions, the wax you skied on yesterday is often faster than the same wax applied today. This is a case when old performs better than new, but it's not a general rule. Check it out where you ski. If it works, use it. We know of more than one race that's been won using the trick, including a couple of recent Olympic Gold Medals.

Second, is the wax in the container new or old? How many months, seasons, or years have gone by since it was made? Is last season's wax still good? Many racers and coaches say no, because up until the late 1950s, most waxes were compounded with natural ingredients, so their properties changed with time on the shelf. But times have changed. Now, all available waxes are compounded from synthetic ingredients so, with proper storage, their shelf life is essentially indefinite. About the only risk we know of involves tubes of klister that have caps off or only partly screwed on. Stored in a warm, humid place (such as in your wax kit tossed into your attic or garage for the summer), they can pick up moisture, which degrades klister properties.

We know of many cases of the opposite situation: of having superb performers in wax we've had for years. But again, this factor is another one of many waxing variables impossible to define in a book. All we can say is try old versus new wax on your skis. We have one favorite Blue kicker wax that, on the tracks where we ski, apparently improves with age when used on marginal snows. So we mark cans, and like vintage wine for honored guests, break them out when the occasion dictates.

Ski Flex

If one pair of skis is softer than another pair, they will grip better because they're easier to flatten against the snow. This is one possible reason why you and a friend can be using the same wax and your skis can be working differently.

Strength and Conditioning

Some skiers are stronger or in better condition than others and are better able to set the wax, or maintain their strength and technique toward the end of a race or workout. Therefore, if everything else is equal, they can get more grip from a given wax than can a weaker skier. Sometimes when our wax slips we know that it's the end of the day's skiing for us. The wax is just fine. It's those bodies that are worn down.

Method of Application

Two skiers can wax with Blue and get different results if one does a poor job of putting it on, or puts it on thicker and longer, or doesn't let it cool long enough, and so on. It pays to be fully aware of waxing methods and tricks.

THE PANIC RACE SITUATION

The start is just a few minutes off and your wax doesn't work. Now what?

If you are using hard wax and need more kick or a softer wax, it's fairly easy to add some outside. Wipe your ski dry with some toweling or terry cloth, and rub on more wax. Then cork it out.

If you are using hard wax and need less kick, you may have to scrape off some of the wax, or shorten the length of the kicker zone by scraping. If your wax is way off, scrape it as clean as you can under the circumstances, and put on a harder wax. Sometimes, with care and skill, you can put a harder wax over a softer one without mixing them too much. But don't count on being able to do it every time.

If you are using klister and need to make an adjustment, times are tough. Usually, after skiing a bit on klister, it gets roughed up, wet, and mixed with dirt. Adding more klister at this point is very difficult. The ideal situation in klister conditions is to have two pair of skis and wax them differently, or have one pair clean and available in the event that you need another wax immediately.

SKI CLEANING

Some of the waxless ski crowd use the necessity to clean skis as another argument against waxing. This may be true, but it depends on how you look at it. Waxless skis also must be cleaned—rightfully enough, less frequently than waxable skis. But the cleaning of a waxless base can be a major undertaking, especially if the waxless pattern (or hair) has become clogged with klister picked up from the track in wet snow conditions. Also, whenever you clean ski bases, you consciously or unconsciously inspect them, noting any damage, which can be fixed before it becomes serious.

When?

Though some skiers regard cleaning skis as an aesthetic exercise, it's no fastidious practice. It's purely practical. We know some good skiers on the citizens' race circuit who apparently never wash their cars and who clean their clothing only slightly more often. But they clean their skis regularly.

We recommend cleaning skis in the following cases:

- The wax on the skis is dirty.
- You want to change categories of wax, from hard wax to klister, or vice versa.
- The base plastic has a whitish surface hue, the telltale sign that it's time for a new round of base preparation.
- You intend to transport the skis, especially in a ski bag or on a car rack.
- You have transported the skis, unbagged, on a car roof-rack for an appreciable distance, say over half-an-hour drive.
- You have finished the day's skiing on klister.
- You intend to store the skis for more than a few days.

How?

There's no set procedure for cleaning skis, but there are a few guidelines:

- **First, remove as much as possible by mechanical means.** Use a good scraper held at a low angle to the base. Some racers carry a putty knife for this purpose. Sometimes you can wipe off warm klister with a rag or balled-up newspaper.

- **Second, remove the rest by other means.** Here you have a choice: chemical wax-dissolving liquid solvents, or heat. We recommend the first, but are personally prone to use the second.

Wax-Dissolving Solvents

These are the most reliable of solvents for ski cleaning. Sold by most major wax makers, they are simply wiped or sprayed on, allowed to work a bit, and wiped off. They are preferable to household or industrial solvents, as they dissolve wax well without damaging thermoplastic ski bases or leaving a residue to which wax won't adhere. Most are also nontoxic and non-flammable.

Heat

Heat is an efficient way to remove both hard wax and klister. Just heat the wax on the ski with a torch flame until the wax melts, then wipe it off with an absorbent rag or tissue. Though simple and direct, the torch-and-wipe method is the most tricky to use. If you let the torch flame play on the base plastic too long, poof!—you have no more ski base. Polyethylene, now the most common base plastic on racing skis, starts to melt at 130°C (266°F), below the temperature recommended for roasting turkey. Remember, if it would singe the bird, it will ruin the base.

A Wipe in Time

The art of ski cleaning lies in wiping at the right instant. When you use chemical cleaner, you should wipe just when the solvent has dissolved the wax. If it evaporates, you'll have a sticky mess on the bases. When you use a torch flame, you should wipe by following the flame, getting off all the molten wax while not running into the wax that's still solid. Always use a lint-free rag (you'll be amazed at how klister will attract even the smallest of lint threads), the ski cleaning tissue marketed by wax makers, or an industrial-grade wiping tissue.

Quick, Easy, and Effective

As much as we truly enjoy caring for our gear, we are continually searching for ways to wax and clean skis quickly. Here are a few tricks we've devised to streamline cleaning:

- **Hard Wax.** If the wax on the skis is clean—the skis have been used in new, cold snow—then you're in business for the one-shot cleaning and preparation game. First, iron more wax onto the whole ski base. Use either old chunks of unidentifiable glide wax, household paraffin, or candles on the glide zones of the base. Use Green cross-country wax on the grip zone underfoot. Iron the wax back and forth. This will cover any bare spots and dilute the old wax you already have on the ski. Follow this by cooling the skis and scraping, using the sharp metal scraper under the foot and on the grip zone, and the plastic scraper on the tip and tail glide zones. The ski is then prepared, ready to be rewaxed. But remember, the trick is good for clean wax only. If you heat dirty wax on the ski, you will fuse dirt into the base, which slows glide.

- **Klister.** While hard wax may last for several kilometers of skiing spread over a number of days, klister should usually be cleaned off skis after every outing. Often, the tip and tail glide zones of the base will pick up klister from both your skis and other skis.

Start every klister removal job by scraping off as much as you can, preferably with a good plastic scraper. Do this job indoors, as cold klister is extremely tenacious stuff. When you're finished scraping, examine the bases.

If there's klister on the tip and tail glide zones, remove it with chemical cleaner. That's the one part of the ski where you definitely don't want to have the stuff. Then repeat the preparation trick just described for hard wax. Or, if you know that you will use klister tomorrow, warm a bit of Blue klister into the grip zone of the base. Blue is a good binder for other klisters; it keeps them from wandering up around the ski side walls or backward along the base.

WAXING AFTER CLEANING

Always rewax freshly cleaned skis with base preparation glide wax or hard cross-country wax. Don't let clean, unwaxed skis stand around for long. Unprotected thermoplastic bases oxidize rapidly, and oxidized bases are slow.

Repeated cleanings and rewaxings condition bases. This is why experienced racers prefer older skis that have been used, cleaned, and rewaxed many times. The reason is simple: Old skis are usually faster.

Cleaning and rewaxing need not be a long, drawn-out process. Once you get the hang of it, you can probably both clean and rewax as you go along. Sometimes you can even do both at once, at least for hard waxes and glide waxes.

7
EQUIPMENT AND CLOTHING

Unless you are well-heeled, you cannot afford to be a cavalier consumer when selecting performance gear. To find what works best for you in racing, you must try, flex, fit, feel, examine, and compare.

Before discussing clothing and equipment particulars, here are five general observations on the available paraphernalia:

- **New models appear almost every season.** Like many consumer goods, sometimes this year's models incorporate significant changes, and sometimes they differ only in cosmetic alterations. Some national team members (who don't pay for their gear) keep a favorite pair of skis for years, using them only in crucial meets. So "new" isn't always "better."

- **Descriptions are usually technical.** Like cars, cross-country ski racing gear is most often described in terms of materials, designs, and constructions. But you don't just control your gear as you do a car. You interact with it so you must either inquire or do some translation to relate technical profiles to performance when you and your gear are out on snow. We do some translation here (see "Recommended Reading" for more information).

- **Trade names outnumber materials.** Worldwide, there are only about a dozen major firms supplying component materials, subassemblies, and parts to the ski equipment industry. There are perhaps no more than twice that many supplying fibers and fabric to the ski garment industry. But trade

---

No Names

At one time, the cross-country product spectrum, including that for racing, was both static and small. Mention the few products that existed, and what was said would be valid for years.

No more. Brand proliferation, changes, takeovers, annual model changes, and the like have made book-mention of brand names a folly.

So we mention brand names and proprietary designs as little as possible. In describing the current boot-binding picture, we have gone just a bit out on a limb because our crystal ball is a bit cloudy in telling us what that part of the gear spectrum will be like when you read this book. Otherwise we have avoided brand names and have even steered clear of mentioning fabrics in clothing. The exceptions are either when a material is extremely common, or a brand name has historical or technical context.

names proliferate, either so various manufacturers may have "exclusives," or to differentiate slight alterations of basic substances.

- **Manufacturer reputation and dealer integrity count.** Ski gear is like baked goods. No matter how excellent the raw materials are, it is the skill with which they are combined, and how the finished product is treated on its way to market, that makes the difference. Even seemingly minor imperfections, such as a haphazardly mounted binding, can destroy the most perfect product.
- **You usually, but not always, get what you pay for.** Generally, gear quality and performance go hand in hand with price. But there are many exceptions. And when you take your own financial needs and skiing abilities into consideration, the absolute ultimate for you is not always the most expensive.

SKIS

In terms of gear, skis are the most decisive item in determining your potential skiing speed. The best of everything else, including duplicates of Olympic team outfits, will not help if you have slow skis. But the opposite is true too: we know of more than one incident when a top racer has had some fun at the expense of a faddish local crowd by showing up at a race clad in hand-me-downs from yesteryear, sporting outdated poles and boots, but shod with a pair of super fast skis. The ridicule at the starting line gets squashed as the body inside the outfit gets the best out of the skis underfoot. Let's face it: the moral of such stories is that it's the skis that count.

Racing skis are faster than recreational cross-country skis of comparable quality for three reasons:
1. They weigh less and have different dimensions and profiles.
2. They have different bases.
3. They have different cambers and stiffnesses.

The first two differences are straightforward and are easy to check out in the ski shop. The third difference is the most important and most frequently neglected aspect.

Dimensions, Weights, and Profiles

One apparent goal of racing ski design is to produce skis as narrow and light as possible. But there are limits.

Ski stability decreases as skis get narrower. So the International Ski Federation (FIS) now stipulates a minimum ski waist width of 44 mm, and most racing skis are made accordingly.

No regulations govern minimum ski weight, but economics and physiology set a lower limit. Skis can be made ultralight by using exotic aerospace materials and by meticulously hand-working critical parts; both increase the price. Also, when skis are too light, the skier gets less feedback, and does not ski as well. Biomechanical tests have been made to determine minimum desirable ski weights, but thus far the results are far from conclusive. Most experienced coaches and racers feel that skis lighter than 1 kg (2 lb, 3 oz) per pair (210-cm length) without bindings would be unmanageable in today's tracks. Finally, ski weight is not as important as, say, jogging or running shoe weight. Very few ski maneuvers demand that you lift the entire ski off the snow; you can easily ski several races or even an entire season without ever doing so. The tips of the skis are almost always on and supported by the snow. As you ski, you can hardly notice small differences in ski weight.

Racing skis are now made only with straight or spear-shaped side profiles. A ski's turning ability depends on a host of parameters, including its side profile. Sidecut, the "hourglass" shape of the side profile when the ski is viewed from above, is a thing of the past in racing skis.

Bases

Various thermoplastics are now used for almost all racing ski bases. Most common are bases of polyethylene, abbreviated PE and marketed under several trade names. Some skis however, have bases of modified ABS (Acrylonitrile Butadiene Styrene) plastic.

Why Sidecut Isn't There

The topic of sidecut and why it isn't on racing skis seems to be a popular subject going the rounds. There are many theories as to why racing skis no longer have sidecut. Two of the more frequently heard reasons involve the use of racing skis in tracks:

1. *Racing skis are used in tracks and therefore need no turning ability, so sidecut can be eliminated.* True, provided the track is good and is there all the time. But have you ever seen perfect tracks for all races for any one season?

2. *With sidecut, skis rub on the sides of the track at tip and tail; straight skis eliminate that rubbing.* If a ski rubs up against the side of a track, what sort of rubbing will slow the ski more, a couple of points or the entire side of the ski? There is no clear-cut answer. Besides, feet are wider than skis, and it's usually binding or boots that rub the sides of the track, not the skis.

These myths aside, there are two other substantial reasons for not having sidecut on racing skis. First, straight sides are far easier to manufacture. Second, all other factors being equal, sidecut or the lack of it has very little effect on the performance of a racing ski. This is because turning and tracking depend not only on side profile, but also on camber flex and stiffness, and on resistance to twist (torsional rigidity).

Lightweight racing skis have relatively stiff cambers and little torsional rigidity compared with other ski types. They simply don't hold their side shape when edged, so they can't be turned by carving, as can alpine skis. In other words, they have no sidecut, because even if they did, it effectively wouldn't be there when ostensibly needed.

Aside from sheer performance (how fast a base is on a ski), you should be interested in its wax-holding ability. How long will your skis perform when waxed well? There's an ongoing debate about the wax-holding properties of base plastics, and the results aren't yet in. You'll probably hear conflicting claims for and explanations of wax-holding ability for years to come.

The simplest explanation of which base plastic holds wax better involves its porosity—the extent to which it is porous. Strictly speaking, this explanation cannot be correct because ski base plastics are impermeable to water. Therefore, they are not porous. But some bases are artificially made with surface voids, or semi-open pores, that fill with wax that is applied to the base.

Wax and plastic scientists postulate that what actually happens when warm wax is applied to a base is that the wax and the surface plastic form a solution, or mix. If this were the entire explanation, bases could be polished mirror-smooth and still hold wax well. But experience says this isn't so. As we said, the results aren't yet in.

Camber

Ski performance is related to camber or how a pair of skis translates the varying forces applied by the skier into varying pressure on the underlying snow. The key word here is *varying*. If the pressure under a pair of skis did not vary, many ski maneuvers would be difficult and some, such as cross-country strides on the flat, would be impossible. Camber is the property that permits kick and glide on skis. If you doubt this, try to ski on a stiff pair of planks, the same dimensions as your skis. You may be able to skate, as if you had giant ice skates on your feet, but you'll get nowhere on the flat or uphill with the planks in a track. In other words, camber is crucial.

A ski's camber stiffness determines the way it exerts pressure on the underlying snow as a result of forces applied by a skier. Camber stiffness is determined mostly by two things: the properties of materials in a ski's structural layers and the positions of these layers in relation to each other.

About Double Camber

The cambers of racing skis differ from those of recreational skis in two important ways. First, racing skis are stiffer to suit faster skiing. It therefore takes more force to flatten the cambers out. Second, skier weight will almost, but not quite, flatten out a correctly matched racing ski camber. There's some camber left as the skier glides. More force is required to flatten out that remaining camber. So racing skis are frequently said to have a second or *double camber*.

The term, however, is misleading. A ski has only one camber. But, that camber can be so structured that the ski becomes stiffer as it flattens out. We prefer the term *camber stiffness*.

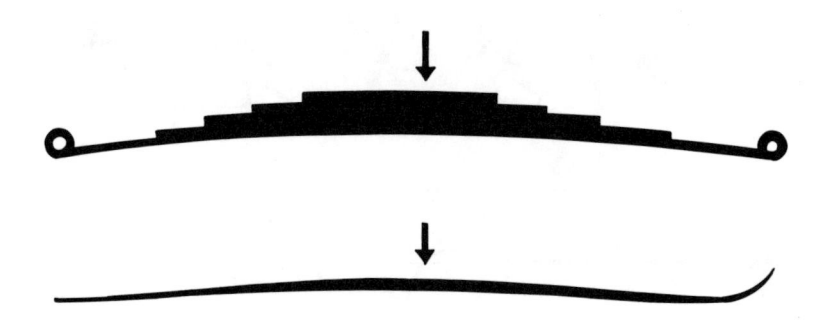

Ski camber stiffness acts like a leaf spring.

Some ski designs rely on core materials to contribute part of camber stiffness, but in most cases core materials play a lesser role.

The ideal performance for a ski's camber is for ski tips and tails to put pressure on the snow during glide while center sections exert pressure only during kicks. How well a ski's camber matches this ideal is determined by how well its properties match the tracks and the skier.

Tracks, and racing ski cambers for them, are usually divided into two categories: wet or klister, and dry or powder. Many ski makers indicate these camber categories by suffixing model numbers with abbreviations such as *K* and *P*.

Wet or klister tracks are usually firm and often very hard, especially if recently packed by heavy machines. Ski grip is usually no problem, but glide can be slow if klister drags. So klister skis have relatively stiff cambers to keep the center sections of the bases up off the snow during glide. This

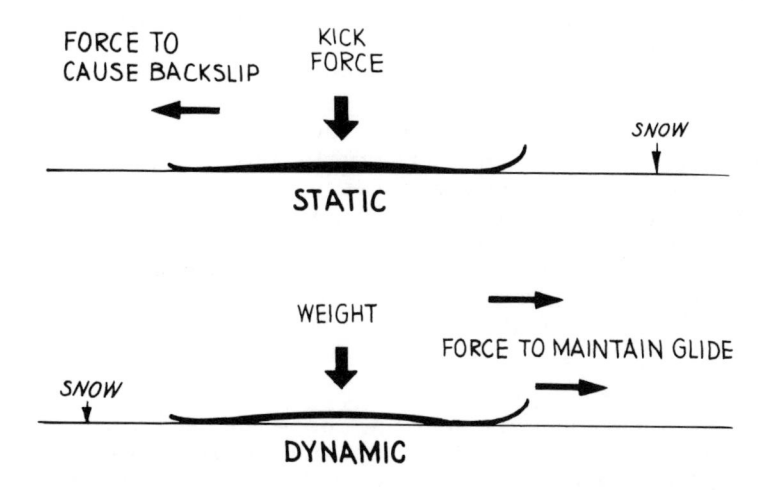

Static underski friction determines grip; dynamic underski friction limits glide.

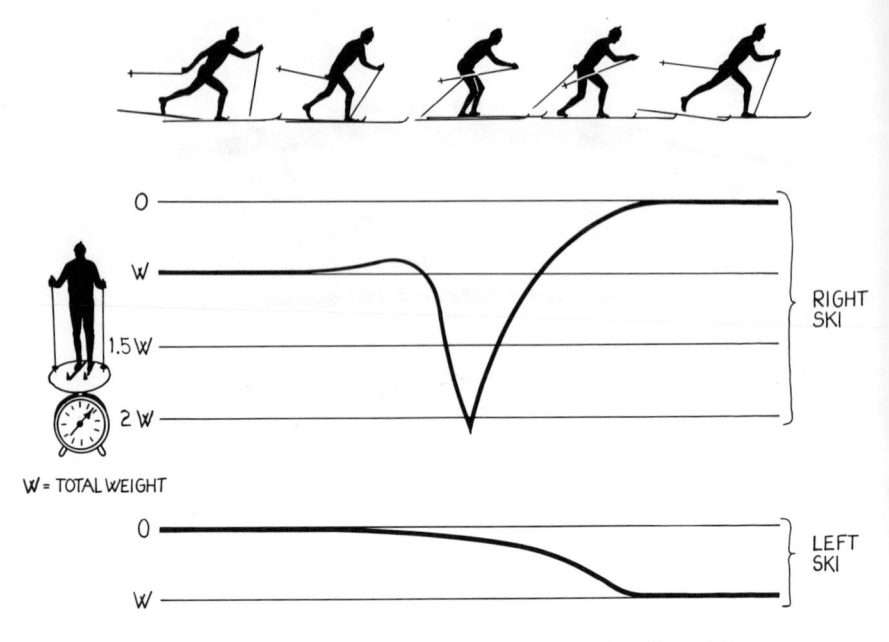

Downward force varies during stride, and is maximum, twice skier weight or more, at the instant of the kick.

takes maximum advantage of the differences in zone waxing for grip and glide (see chapter 6).

Dry or powder tracks are usually softer than wet-snow tracks, and may actually give way under a ski. Ski grip is usually no problem, except at temperatures just at freezing. Glide is slowed only at very low temperatures. therefore powder skis have longer camber curves that spread out the center grip-waxed section. Because most hard cross-country grip waxes actually glide fairly well, the transition between the grip and glide portions of the camber is not as sharp as for klister skis. This is why powder skis are softer than klister skis for the same skier.

If you cannot afford to buy two pairs of racing skis, select a pair that matches the prevailing snow conditions where you most frequently race. Or buy a compromise pair—usually powder skis that are just on the stiff side of what you would ideally select for soft tracks.

Fiber Facts

Modern cross-country racing skis owe their strength and many performance characteristics to materials hidden in the layers just under the top sheet. It is these structural layers, which like the arch of a bridge, form the vital framework of the ski.

In each structural layer are bundles made up of thousands of tiny fiber filaments. They are held in place by a plastic such as epoxy. These are the strong fibers that give the layer, and therefore the ski, its major characteristics. The most commonly used fibers are fiberglass, carbon fiber, and aramid fiber.

Fiberglass is by far the most common of the three. Fiberglass-reinforced plastic (often abbreviated FRP) has been used since the 1930s for products such as pleasure boat hulls, shipping containers, and, more recently, for automobile body parts. Because fiberglass has been around for many years, the technology for using it is well developed and widespread. A broad range of fiberglass materials and laminates are available to the ski maker.

Carbon, or graphite (after the material) fiber, marketed under trade names such as Grafil, is three times as stiff and 60 percent stronger than fiberglass. It was originally developed in the mid-1960s for aircraft structures. But it is now most widely used in ultralightweight sports equipment, such as tennis rackets, hockey sticks, golf clubs, ski poles, and skis. Compared with fiberglass, carbon fiber is a more expensive raw material. Because it is stiffer, it is also more brittle, making it more difficult to use in production. That further increases the cost of finished products.

Aramid fibers, marketed under trade names such as Kevlar, like carbon fiber, were developed for aerospace applications. They are 40 percent lighter and two to three times as strong as fiberglass. Compared with carbon fiber,

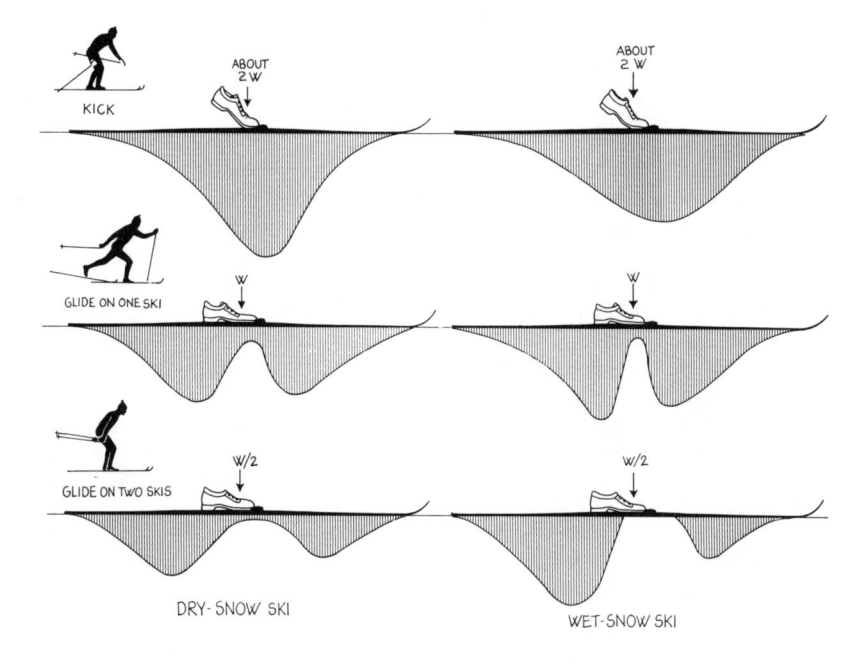

Dry-snow and wet-snow skis are designed to put different pressures on the underlying snow.

they tend to damp forces applied, similar to the way shock absorbers damp the forces applied to automobile springs. Along with their light weight and high strength, this property has led to their use in products where mechanical shocks are involved. These include offshore racing powerboat hulls, safety helmets, and bulletproof vests. When unweighted, an aramid-fiber ski will stay on the snow for a brief instant longer than a carbon-fiber ski. Many racers feel that this slight lag gives better control of ski grip.

Skillfully used in ski design and manufacture, the exotic properties of carbon and aramid fibers can result in lighter, higher-performance skis. They are, however, more expensive than fiberglass skis. But since less than a tenth of a ski is actually fibers, good designs in fiberglass skis often can compete in weight, and certainly in price, with the more expensive materials.

Picking a Good Pair of Skis

The primary rule for selecting skis is to start with the right length. But with cross-country racing skis, there are so many modifications that length is just a starting point. A ski should be long enough to reach to the wrist or palm of an upraised arm. This means that skis are about 30 cm (a foot) longer than body height for average adult males, and 25 cm (10 in.) longer than body height for average adult females.

- **Camber is more important than ski length.** Most ski makers increase camber stiffness with ski length to match the tendency for body weight to increase with height. So a short, stocky racer may have to select longer skis

Who's Skinny?

You sometimes may see or hear the term *skinny skis* applied to cross-country skis in general, and sometimes *toothpicks* applied to cross-country racing skis. You won't find the terms used in this book.

Cross-country ski gear has evolved steadily through the years, becoming lighter as superior lightweight materials, better glues, better fabrics, and more precise production methods have become available. It has been a natural process of a sport benefiting from technology.

It's alpine ski gear that has changed. After *alpine skiing* split from *skiing*, its equipment grew heavier to better suit its unidirectional purpose. The trend accelerated after lifts were built so skiers no longer had to supply their own power. In comparison to its parent, alpine gear got fat.

What if cross-country skiing were the norm in North America when alpine skiing suddenly flowered in the early 1970s? Would skiers then refer to the newcomers on the equipment scene as *obese skis*? Would an alpine racer, complete with boots almost up to his knees become the *hippo* of the sport?

To get stiff enough skis, a stocky racer may select long skis, while a slender racer may select short skis.

to find a pair with enough camber stiffness, while a tall, thin racer may have to select shorter skis to find a pair that is soft enough.

• **Contact length is more important than imprinted length.** Ski contact length (the length of the base that contacts a flat underlying snow surface) is more important than the length imprinted on a pair of skis. Skis having different imprinted lengths may have the same contact length, and vice versa.

• **Body build and skiing style count.** If you have long legs for your height and take long strides, you may prefer a longer ski. This helps you to avoid

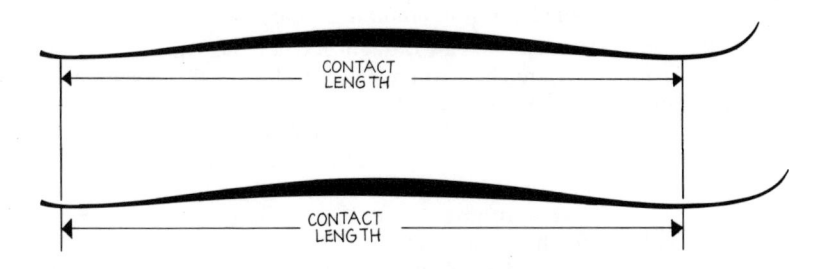

Contact length can be the same, although imprinted ski lengths differ.

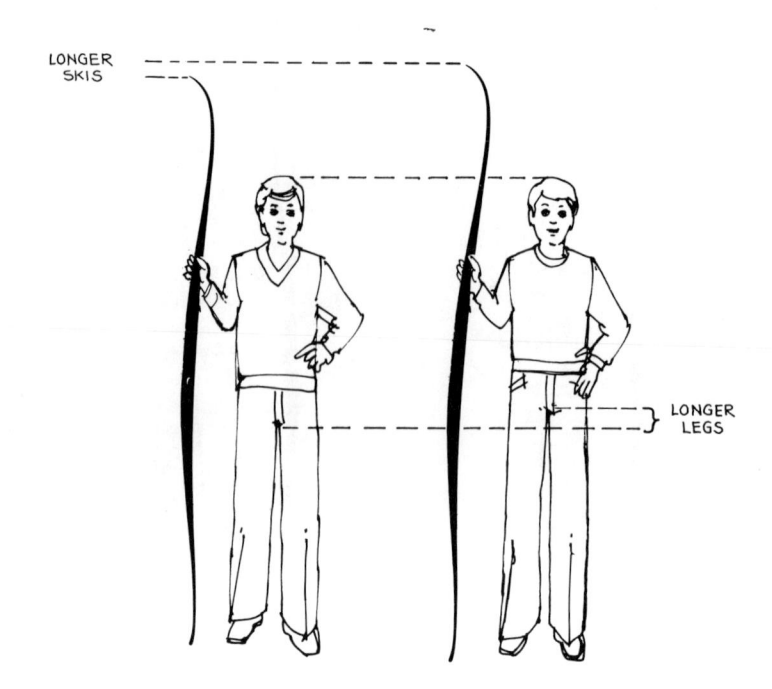

Long-legged racers may have longer strides and feel more comfortable with longer skis.

inadvertently running the tip of one ski in behind the boot of the opposite ski. Conversely, if you have short legs for your height and take shorter, high-tempo strides, you may prefer a shorter ski that you can whip back and forth more quickly.

- **There's no standard for imprinted lengths.** Skis of the same imprinted length from different makers aren't always equally long. This is because there are at least three ways to measure the length imprinted on a ski. In extreme cases, actual lengths of different brands can vary by as much as 5 cm for a 210-cm ski. So don't be surprised if you have to go up or down a few centimeters when switching from brand X to brand Y.
- **Where you race can have some influence.** If you race mostly on gradual courses with long, flat stretches, you may want a longer ski for stability. But if you race mostly on courses in thickly wooded areas with choppy terrain, where the course profiles resemble a cross between sawteeth and a corkscrew and the course map looks like yarn the cat played with on the living room floor, then you'll probably tend to favor shorter skis. These will ease the herringboning, skate turning, quick direction and inclination changes you must make throughout the race.

There's only one way to find the right length. Ski and see. But remember, in racing, a good camber is your best friend. Start there.

Many skis are imprinted with symbols indicating camber stiffness. These symbols are keyed to selection charts that index skier weight and ability to powder-ski and klister-ski stiffnesses. There are also testers that do the same job, ranging from a hand-held C-clamp fitted with a pressure gauge, to fancier units with dials and lights that show ski contact along a flat surface. All these approaches are good guides, but none is absolute. When these selection systems fail, it is for the same reason that any system based on averages fails: nobody is "average." So while you will find the numbers game in camber selection useful, you shouldn't necessarily believe it without question.

You should always hand test camber, no matter how well the manufacturer's numbers or the shop tester seems to match the skis to you. Would you buy a guitar or piano without ever playing a note?

One way to check camber is with the paper test. You can ask to do it in the shop. It is a useful guide for selecting camber stiffness, but it's not the ultimate judge. Properly done, however, it will tell you if ski cambers are dead wrong for you.

Start the paper test by placing a sheet of paper or 3-by-5-in. file card under the middle of one ski. The ski should rest on a flat, horizontal, clean, uncarpeted floor. Stand with body weight equally divided between the two skis, with your shoe tips at the ski balance points. With proper camber stiffness for most citizens' racing, the paper or file card can be moved back and forth for at least the length of your foot under the ski. With all your weight on one ski, the paper or card should be clamped firmly, so that you can barely wiggle it, but you can't pull it out from under the ski without tearing it.

The paper test has drawbacks, and chances are you don't need it if you have been skiing for awhile: you know how your skis feel and perform on snow. That's your best index for selecting camber.

Another way to test for proper camber is with your hands. If you're fit enough to run a citizens' race, then your arm strength should be proportional to your overall body and leg strength. What you can do with your hands tells you something about what you can do with your legs.

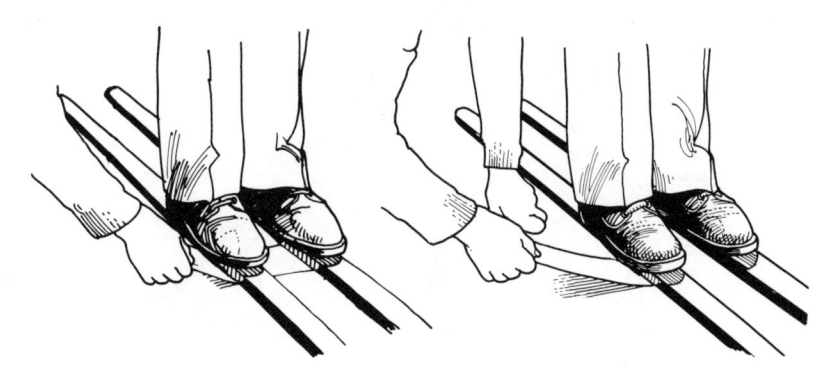

The paper test is a good check for camber.

Start by holding a pair of skis in your hands at their midpoints, base to base. If you can squeeze the bases together to within a sixteenth-of-an-inch or so with one hand, the camber is about right for a dry-snow ski for you. If you can close the bases completely with one hand, they are too soft for racing use. For klister skis, you should just barely be able to close the bases together using two hands, but not one.

While you are hand testing cambers, check for ski defects that can affect performance. Some defects, such as cosmetic blemishes, are unimportant. (If you are good at bargaining though, you might get a discount if you find them.) The defects that can affect performance are twist, warp, pair mate, pair closure, and base flatness.

- **Twist and warp.** These defects will cause skis to wander and yaw, that is, climb out of instead of run in a track. Check for twist by holding a pair of skis together, with bases just touching at tip and tail. Sight them from tail to tip. The bases should touch over their entire widths at the shovel. If there is a V-shaped gap, one or both skis is twisted. Even if there is no gap, both skis may be twisted in different directions. Check for this defect by reversing one ski, pairing the skis up tail-to-tip, and resighting. Check for warp by holding the skis base-to-base with tips and tails well aligned. Squeeze midpoints together. They should meet exactly. If they don't, one or both skis is warped. Even if they meet exactly, both skis may be warped in opposite

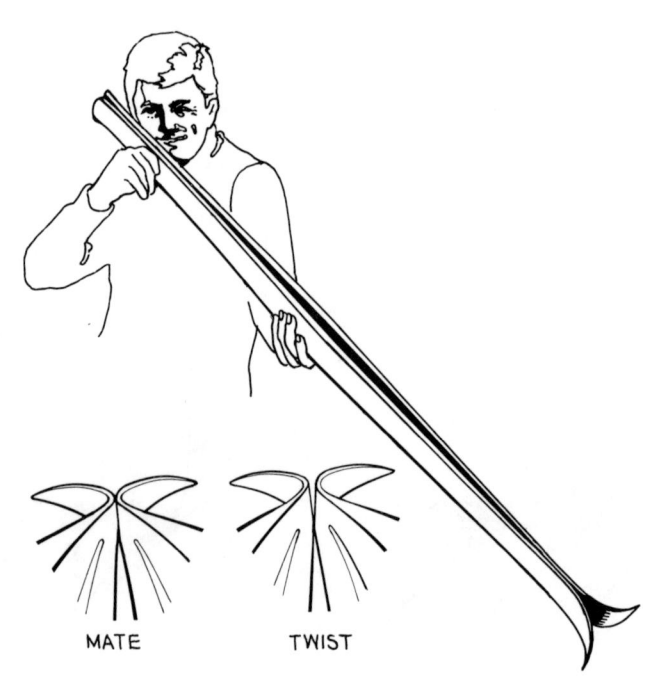

Sight along skis to check for twist.

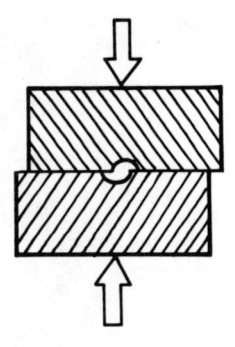

Mid-ski mismate indicates warp.

directions. Again, check for this defect by reversing one ski and repeating the test.

- **Mate and closure.** You can check mate and closure at the same time you check twist. Sight between the bases, from tails toward tips, as you squeeze the pair together at their midpoints. The bases should close evenly and smoothly, with no high or low points and no gaps between the points where the bases touch. Bumpy bases wear wax unevenly and glide poorly. With the skis held completely together, sight along the line where the edges meet on both sides of the skis. The lines should be straight. If they are bowed in one direction, toward one ski of the pair, that ski is stiffer. Then rest both skis on a flat surface, side by side with bases down. Their centers should be equally high. Alternately press both skis down to double-check that they are equally stiff.
- **Base flatness.** Bases can be rounded in two ways. Convex or bowed bases, commonly caused by wear on old skis, wobble in tracks and wear wax unevenly. Concave or railed bases wear wax unevenly and degrade wax grip. Slight curvatures, up to a few tenths-of-a-millimeter (about 0.01 in.) across a 44-mm-wide racing ski base, have little effect. You can correct greater curvatures with sandpaper, but why buy a job with the skis when

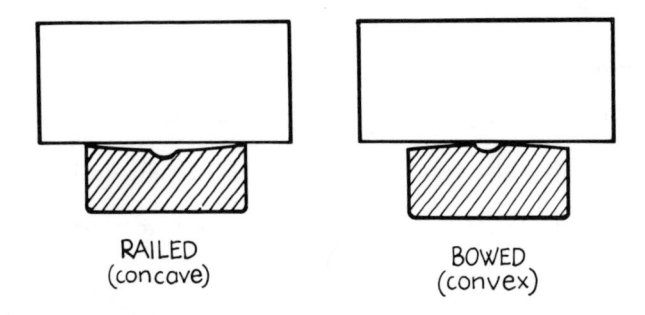

RAILED (concave)

BOWED (convex)

Check base flatness with a straightedge.

The Norwegian Birkebeiner start from Rena is a continuous climb.
(J. Klassen photo)

you can find a better pair? Check base flatness by placing a steel base scraper or other good straightedge on the base. Sight along the base against a light. If you see wedges of light at the center around the tacking groove, the base is railed. If you see openings at the edges and you can rock the straightedge, the base is bowed.

Final Words to the Wise

As we discuss in chapter 6 on "Waxing," cross-country racing glide has recently been overemphasized at the expense of grip. The fad has not only started some racers off on the wrong waxing foot, but also has landed them on the wrong skis.

The most common error has been to buy skis that are too stiff, and that trend has started a vicious circle. More stiff skis are sold, so dealers stock more and factories produce more. In some shops that's all you'll find: skis that are too stiff. There are three reasons why you should avoid them:

1. Stiff skis are unforgiving. You may be able to punch their cambers

down for grip at the start of a race, but will your kick be just as strong in the second and third hour of a distance race? Stiff skis will tire you more quickly.

2. Stiff skis backslip more, especially on uphills. Even top racers cannot always flatten out stiffer ski cambers on uphills. This is why, despite superior modern course preparation, you see far more herringboning on uphills than was the case just a few years ago.

3. Stiff skis are less stable on downhills. They wander and cut up out of tracks more readily than softer skis. If you doubt this, squeeze a pair of downhill racing skis or jumping skis (on big hills, jumpers often land at 60 mph) that are obviously built for stability at speed. Compared with cross-country racing skis, they have noodle cambers. The conclusion is obvious: Stiff skis up the risk of spills on hills.

If you already have skis that are just slightly too stiff, you can correct the problem somewhat. Wax more layers of softer wax for a kicker than you normally would for the snow involved. While this will counter backslip, it will not give you more oomph to kick in the third hour of a race or enhance stability on downhills. Those curses will still be with you.

Skis that are too soft tend to wear grip or kicker wax quickly, because center sections drag more on the snow. But if you have soft skis and fear wax wear in a long race, just wax accordingly and start with a good binder. Remember, a medium- or soft-cambered ski isn't a dead ski; it's just less demanding and more forgiving.

Be Kind To Your Underfoot Friends

In the days of wooden skis, racers did everything possible to avoid running ski tips into things. They knew that they shouldn't risk damage at the ski's weakest point. Fiberglass skis are far stronger at the tips, but do have a weak point right in middle. They're not indestructible. Use a ski for a trampoline in a dip at the bottom of a steep hill and you risk popping the laminations right off the core. You may not notice the damage immediately but it will spread as you ski. Then later, in some apparently innocent maneuver, the ski will break. What gets blamed? You've guessed it: the ski. There you were on a good flat track, and the darned thing just broke!

Cyclists don't expect the tires and wheels of expensive ten-speeders to hold up when they ride full tilt into a pothole. And even the best dress shoes will rapidly fall apart if you use them on a mountain backpacking trip.

But often common sense gets tossed out the window when less skilled skiers buy and use skis. They start by buying the ultimate in a lightweight performance ski, and then ski on it as if it were a robust snowshoe.

Skiers, especially racers, should be kind to their skis. Love your skis, and they'll serve you well.

BOOTS AND BINDINGS

Judging from what you see in ski shops, the unemployed mousetrap designers of the world must have switched to devising cross-country boots and bindings.

Even before the newer boot-binding systems hit the market for the 1976 season, there were close to forty different bindings in the Nordic Norm system. Many of these bindings were marketed with extraordinary claims of exclusive, superior features. No matter how you looked at that situation, it was nothing more than an excessive number of ways to hold a cross-country ski boot in place.

Now there are six competing boot-binding systems to choose from (at the rate new systems appear, there may be six more by the time you read this book). No system is fully compatible with another. This may sound worse than the situation prior to 1976, but actually it's an improvement. Competition has resulted in true progress.

The basic principle of all current boot-binding systems has not changed from the traditional recipe. The boot toe attaches to a simple toe binding that is mounted on the ski. This binding correctly locates the boot with respect to the ski balance point. The systems differ chiefly in the manner of boot attachment.

We'll discuss the old standby Nordic Norm, and the three others most commonly used in racing. In order of appearance on the market, they are: Norm 38, Racing Norm, and Salomon. Their major features are compared in the table opposite.

Functionally, the systems divide into three groups:

- **Welt clamp.** The traditional Nordic Norm usually has a binding bail that fits on top of the boot welt at the toe. The line of flex, or hinging is just under the forward edge of the boot upper. Because fixation is around the welt at the toe and the binding sidepieces extend along the sides of the sole, there is a right and left binding. Nordic Norm bindings are not seen much in classified racing, but are fully usable for citizens' racing.

- **Snout clamp.** The Norm 38 and Racing Norm fix an extension, or snout, on the boot sole at its toe into the binding. The flex, or hinge, is forward of the front edge of the boot upper. Bindings are symmetrical; no right or left.

- **Snout device.** The Salomon boot toe is fitted with a special metal device that mates with a tongue on the binding mechanism. The flex, or hinge, is located on that mechanism. Bindings are symmetrical; no right or left.

It All Began with the Rat Trap

The Nordic Norm system descends from the first basic pin binding, the Rottefella (Norwegian word for "rat trap"), which has been around since 1928. The boot toe is held by an overlapping bail that presses the sole down onto protruding pins. The pins lock into sole recesses. Subsequent modifications of the basic system include pins going down into the welt of the boot sole, and spikes protruding completely through the sole. Nordic Norm pin bindings are now available in a spectrum of designs in both metal and

BOOT-BINDING SYSTEMS

SYSTEM	BINDING HOLDS BOOT AT/BY:	WIDTH AT ATTACH-MENT	SOLE THICK-NESS	BINDING MATERIAL	FRONT EDGE OF BOOT UPPER LOCATES:* Ahead of rear screws	FRONT EDGE OF BOOT UPPER LOCATES:* Behind front screw	COMMENTS
Nordic Norm	Clamping welt in front of boot upper	75 mm	12 mm	Metal or Plastic	25 mm	22 mm	"Old Reliable." Many models. Many makers. Has right and left binding.
Norm 38	Clamping rectangular snout on sole	38 mm	7 mm	Metal or Plastic	14.5 mm	32.5 mm	Adidas exclusive. Some licensees also offer models. Symmetrical binding.
Racing Norm	Clamping tapered snout on sole	50 mm	7 mm	Metal	12 mm	35 mm	Not patented. Several makers. Many models. Symmetrical binding.
				Plastic	24 mm	23 mm	
Salomon	Latch onto metal tongue holds rectangular clevis on sole	30 mm	7 mm	Plastic with some metal parts	9 mm	36 mm	Salomon exclusive. Some license production of boots by other makers. Symmetrical binding.

*Note: Bindings of all systems mount with the same triangular configuration of three screws, a single forward screw located 47 mm ahead of the centerline of two rear screws, whose centers are 26 mm apart. The distances listed show where the boot locates with respect to these three screws, and therefore indicate how much boots might move forward or back on skis should you change boot-binding systems and use the same mounting holes. The distances listed are typical only; exact distances vary according to make and model of binding.

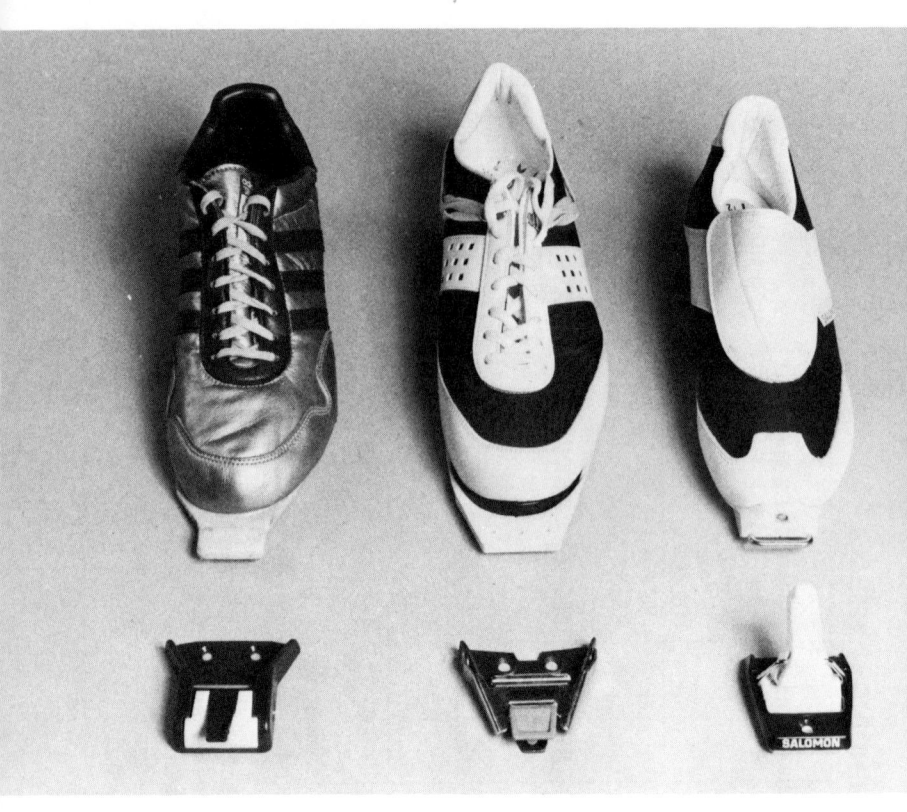

Norm 38, Racing Norm, and Salomon boot-binding systems. (Fletcher Manley photo)

plastic. Many are light enough for racing. (These were the only bindings used before the newer snout boot-binding systems appeared in 1976.) Despite the multitude of available Nordic Norm boots and bindings, all bindings fit all boots. That is the point of the Nordic Norm standard. There are three standard widths, measured at the pins of the binding or pin recesses of the boot: 71, 75, and 79 mm, with 75 mm being by far the most common and now the only width used for racing models. Nordic Norm boot soles are 12 mm thick and are usually made of vulcanized rubber or an expanded plastic material.

The break with the tried-and-true rat trap system came in the 1975–76 season, when Adidas of France introduced the first snout-type boots and toe-clip bindings. Many winning racers used them in the 1976 Winter Olympic cross-country races in Seefeld, Austria. Rottefella soon followed suit, with the Racing Norm, a design based on a down-scaling of the Nordic Norm. Both the Adidas Norm 38 and the Racing Norm fix boots to bindings by holding a sole snout extension. The boot soles are made of hard plastic for lateral stability, and are thin (just 7 mm or slightly less than one-quarter inch) for ease of forward foot flex. The systems differ in the shape of the boot sole snout and the binding, and the method by which the snout is held to the binding. The width of the Racing Norm system at the point of attachment is 50 mm, and boot sole thickness is 7 mm. They are sometimes referred to as "50/7." A thicker-soled (12 mm instead of 7 mm) version of the Racing Norm, called the Touring Norm, is also available. The thicker soles are intended to insulate better. As you might expect, the system is termed "50/12." The Norm 38 is an Adidas exclusive, with a few models of bindings being made under license by other makers, such as Geze. The Racing Norm system is not patented, so Racing Norm boots and bindings are available from several makers.

The Salomon system involves fitting a rectangular metal clevis on the boot toe to a metal tongue on the binding. The clevis is held in place by a plastic lever, and the boot sole hinge point is not in the sole itself, but in a flexible binding insert. This insert is offered in three stiffnesses to suit different skiing kick powers. They are identified by color: red, softest; white, medium; blue, stiffest. The system is patented and produced by Salomon of France, with some firms in other countries producing boots to fit the system under license.

Which One?

In any citizens' race, you'll see the entire spectrum of boot-binding systems in use. And with the exception of factory-team racers, who are obligated to use specific products, you'll see no correlation between placings on result lists and boot-binding systems. Almost everything goes.

It is commonly believed that the major advantage of newer boot-binding systems over racing versions of the Nordic Norm is light weight. The boots are indeed lighter, but generally that light weight is achieved at the expense of overall insulation, meaning they are colder. So skiers wear more socks or use overboots, or both. Then they have the added weight of extra socks and overboots.

The newer systems do have other advantages over the Nordic Norm. First, they are symmetrical: there is no right or left to the bindings. So you can freely swap your skis or swap with another skier without worrying about the correct foot match. Second, their stiffer soles provide better lateral control of light racing skis, and some models have guiding devices to assure constant boot-ski alignment. Lateral control is of little advantage when you diagonal stride in a firm track, but is important whenever you skate, steer your skis through a turn, or herringbone uphill. Finally, the newer systems are kinder on the toes. The Nordic Norm boot-binding fixation just at the welt often caused folds in the boot just over the toes. In the old days, you could always tell cross-country ski racers from all other athletes: they were the ones with blue toenails.

We're not knocking the Nordic Norm system. It's great. And it'll probably be around for a long while, especially for recreational skiing. You can't beat the boots for general utility on skis and off (try driving a small imported car wearing fancy snout boots and you'll see what we mean). If you feel comfortable with Nordic Norm boots and racing bindings, why change?

But if you want some of the advantages offered by the newer systems, check them out to see which one best suits your needs. If you switch boot-binding systems, however, be prepared to switch skis. Unfortunately, the systems do not have compatible binding locations, and drilling more than one set of binding holes in cross-country racing skis is not a good idea. In fact, the limited ski guarantees offered by some ski makers are invalidated if more than three holes are drilled in the topsheet.

Now, which model is for you? It depends. Here are our priorities:

1. First and foremost, find a boot that fits. A wide variety of lasts (models of the human foot on which boots are shaped) are used in making boots. Even boots made by one firm may fit differently. When trying on boots, walk a bit, flexing your foot fully forward as in the diagonal stride. Reject any boot that's uncomfortable at the toes. Discomfort in the shop will probably translate to misery on skis. If other parts of your anatomy hurt, you can usually continue to ski. But if your feet hurt badly, you have to stop.

2. Pick a system that is sold and serviced where you live or ski. Boot snouts or attachment devices can fail, and bindings can be damaged, especially in transport. Don't let a minor problem stop you from skiing.

3. Pick a system that performs well for you. In other words, ski and see. Try out a system before you buy. No two systems perform exactly the same. Some highly skilled racers can switch systems, ski a bit, and automatically adjust. Most of us, however, are less fortunate. It takes time to adapt to a new underfoot flex, a new hinge point, and a different guide of boot onto ski as the foot comes forward in strides. Pick the system that feels the best, the one to which you feel you can adapt most rapidly.

4. Check the binding baseplate. That is the flat part that screws onto the ski. All bindings mount with three screws in a triangle. But standard screw spacing doesn't mean that all baseplates mount equally well. As you ski, your boots apply forces that tend to rock the bindings back and forth on the skis. This action stresses screws upward and digs the front and rear edges of the baseplates down into ski top sheets. Longer baseplates result in less upward pull on the screws and less downward dig of edges. Short baseplates, where edges just clear mounting screw heads, maximize upward pull on screws and downward edge dig. Avoid metal bindings with sharp edges. They can fracture the ski top sheets.

5. Check how wear might affect boot-binding fit. If wear could degrade fit and cause boots to be loose in bindings, look for binding adjustments to compensate for the wear. The problem is particularly acute with the Racing Norm system. Good designs of these bindings incorporate a feature that pulls the boot farther forward. This compensates for wear because it increases sole snout clearance against the binding side pieces.

6. Think of how much you walk in the boots. Plastic soles are slippery unless fitted with rubber inserts under the ball of the foot and heel. Look for these inserts, because they are useful in walking and cannot hinder skiing performance. We know of more than one racer who has returned from a race bruised or injured—not from skiing, but from slipping on steps while dashing to the rest room.

```
         BINDING         BOOT
```

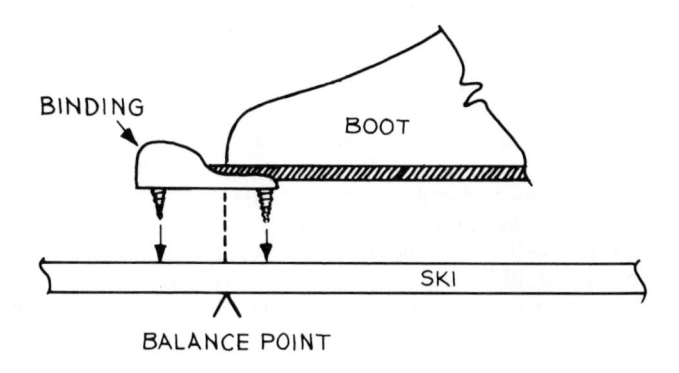

(figure: binding and boot mounted on ski, with arrows indicating screw positions above the BALANCE POINT of the SKI)

"Where do you mount bindings?" translates into "Where do you locate binding screws so boots position correctly on skis?" The best average mounting is one that places the front edge of the boot upper just over the ski balance point.

7. Check sole and heel plates. These devices, usually made of plastic, mount behind the binding. They have ridges that mate with corresponding recesses in the boot sole and heel. Some have protrusions that dig into a softer part of the heel to guide the boot and hold it on the ski. Most models supplied with bindings work well. But you should avoid the extreme accessory versions that are designed to aid turning in cross-country downhill skiing. They are of no use in racing. There are too many of these devices to list, but there is one thing you should look for when evaluating them: the holes necessary to mount them on your skis should be as few, and as small, as possible. Most racing ski designs incorporate a reinforcement laminate just where the three holes will be bored. But ski makers cannot predict the type or location of sole and heel plates to be mounted. So there's usually no extra reinforcement behind the binding mount area. Bore big holes or pound in lots of nails here, and you risk damage to the ski structure. This invites ski failure. Ski makers, in fact, list this type of damage as the leading cause of racing ski fracture and failure. Therefore, if ski makers offer any guarantee on their products, they usually specifically exclude coverage for failures due to this cause. Look for devices that are gentle to your skis. One current, acceptable design combines a self-adhesive patch on the sole/heel plate for secure location, plus a few small brass brads for attachment.

POLES

Traditionally, poles are fourth in line in discussions of ski gear hardware. For many skiers, that's also the rank of their importance.

Though rarely in the limelight of skier equipment interest, poles are vital. Have you ever noticed what part of your anatomy seems to tire first, especially on the first few training tours of a season? Your arms. And what item of equipment do you always use for forward thrust in all ski strides? Your poles. Your arms and poles work together, supplying from 10 to 25 percent of your forward power. In terms of what they can do for you, good poles are important.

Racing poles compare with recreational poles in the same way that racing and recreational skis compare. Racing poles are lighter and more slender than recreational poles just as racing skis are the lightest and most slender of the cross-country ski spectrum. Racing poles are stiffer than recreational poles and can better transmit arm power to packed snow surfaces, just as racing skis have stiffer cambers for fast in-track skiing. Racing poles have half baskets for push only on the packed snow of racing tracks, just as racing skis have straight sides for in-track use only. Finally, like racing skis, racing pole construction involves more exotic, and therefore more expensive, materials than does recreational equipment.

Picking a Pole

A pole seems the ultimate of simplicity. It is just a grip handle, rod, and a basket or protrusion that keeps it from sinking into the snow. That simplicity is deceiving because poles have interrelated characteristics that are important in racing. The essential performance characteristics of poles are weight, stiffness, balance, and handling.

Weight. Unlike skis, poles seem to have no minimum desirable weight. A pole is simply an extension of your hand. All other things equal, the lighter the pole, the less it will tire your hand and arm. Today's lightest poles weigh about 140 gr (4.9 oz) each in a 140-cm length, or about 10 gr (0.35 oz) per 10 cm of pole length. Good weights for racing range up to about 14.5 gr (0.5 oz) per 10 cm of pole length.

- **Stiffness.** In the past it was felt that racing poles should have whippy shafts that would give a little as baskets troweled snow back and forth. You'll find statements to that effect in our respective earlier books. But times have changed. Racers no longer charge off into the wilderness; they compete on packed courses. So racers now strive for maximum feel in precise poling, and that requires stiff shafts. The stiffer the shaft and the less it bends when you push on the grip, the better.

- **Balance.** If you are accustomed to wielding any implement in your hand—a hammer, baseball bat, or fly rod—you know that some have a good feel and some do not. That feeling isn't necessarily related to their weight. Some heavier implements may feel better than their lighter counterparts. That feel usually has to do with balance.

In poling, balance is noted most in the forward arm swing when the pole acts like a pendulum attached to your hand. The closer the pole balance point to your hand, the less it will tend to swing by itself and the more it will do as you direct. The theoretically perfect pole would have a balance point right at your hand. A flick of the wrist and, presto, the basket would be just where you want it. Think of those times when your pole baskets pick up snow when you ski in wet, sticky conditions. It doesn't take much snow collected on the baskets to ruin your arm coordination and force you to stop and shake it off. Good racing poles have the balance considerably closer to the grip than to the tip end of the pole; 45 percent of pole length from the grip end is common. Poles with balance points closer to tip than grip ends

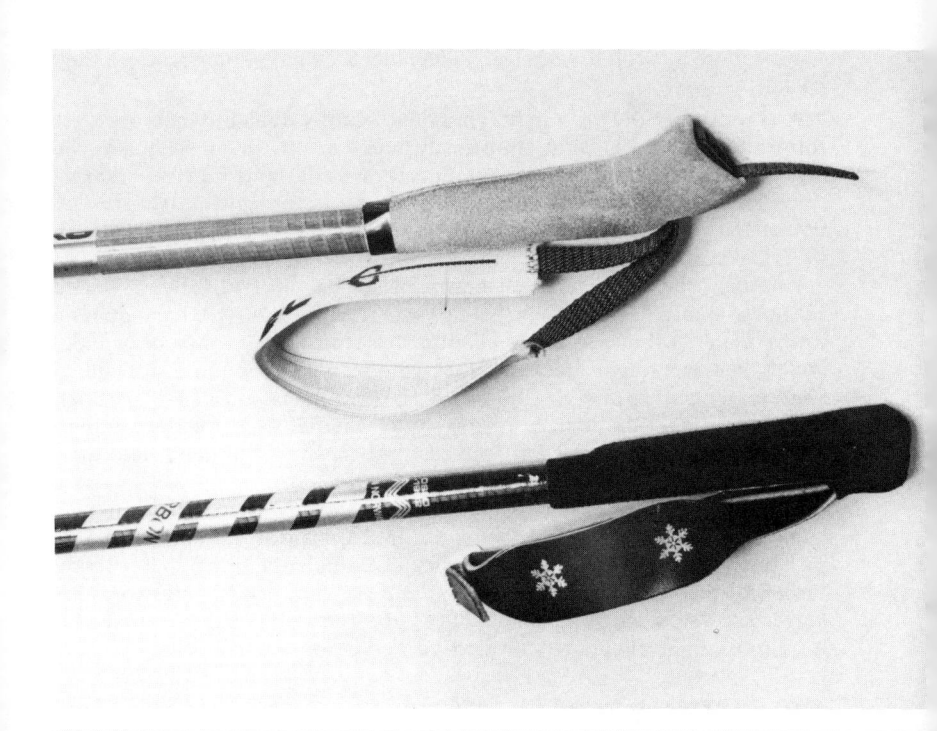

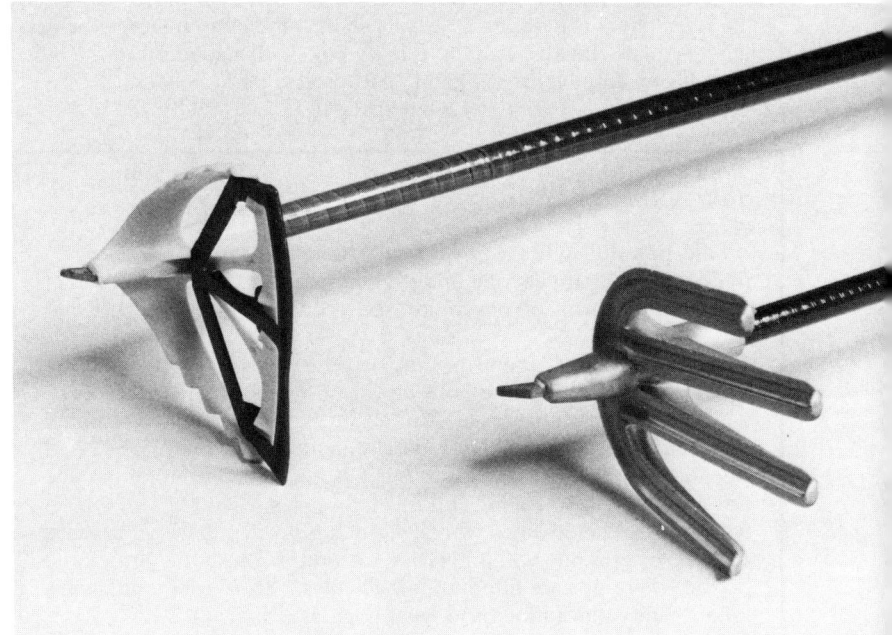

Two common approaches to grip and basket design for racing poles, the Norwegian and the Finnish. (Fletcher Manley photo)

will be more difficult to use. They'll feel like they have snow stuck to their baskets.

- **Handling.** How the grip fits your hand is individual. But there are a few things to look for: (1) Is the strap easily adjustable, with a mechanism you can operate outdoors when your fingers are cold and you are wearing mittens? (2) Is the strap long enough to fit around your hand and wrist when you are wearing thick gloves or mittens? (3) Does the grip fit your hand well in all the poling positions?

Another aspect of handling is how well tips bite into snow throughout a season of skiing. This requires that tips stay sharp in use, and that requires a tough material. Snow is, after all, abrasive stuff. Best are tips of carbide, which has the single drawback that when dulled, it's more difficult to sharpen than other materials. But with a little care, that job is easy (see box). Hardened steel tips, usually of the same material used for the studs in studded snow tires, work well, are easily sharpened, but don't hold their edge as long as carbide tips.

Finally, there is the basket. All racing poles are now fitted with asymmetrical baskets that protrude to the rear from the shaft. In selecting a basket, pick one with a tight enough web (or small enough openings) so it will ride on top of the snow in the area where you ski. You need tighter webs for looser snows. Some pole makers offer clip-on attachments so basket performance can be altered to suit hard-packed or loose pole tracks.

A Pole Is Mostly Shaft

The most obvious part of a pole is its shaft—the long, hollow tube from which it is made. If you buy a top-quality pole with a good shaft, the other parts will probably be just as good. With poles, perhaps more than with other items of ski gear, you get what you pay for.

Sharpening Pole Tips

Pole tips dull with use, especially when used on crust and icy tracks, or when they strike underlying rocks, dirt, or asphalt. Roller ski poles, used only on pavement, seem constantly afflicted with dull tips.

Touching up tips whenever they become dulled is routine maintenance that will save time both on and off skis. Sharpen tips on a whetstone or grinding wheel. Aluminum oxide stones and wheels are adequate for sharpening hard metal pole tips. You'll need a vitrified silicon carbine stone or wheel ("green wheel") however, for carbide tips on high-quality racing and roller ski poles. Grind tips wet, from both sides. When using a wheel, quench tips often in water, because the heat of grinding will otherwise loosen the glue bond or melt the plastic where tips are fitted to pole ferrules. When grinding, always follow safety precautions and wear goggles.

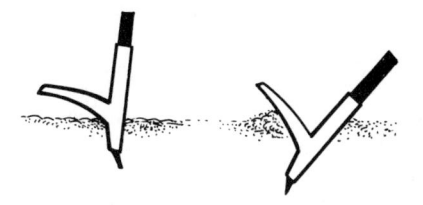

Asymmetrical baskets ease poling on hard-packed racing tracks.

Materials used for pole shafts seem to have their heydays. Natural tonkin cane was long king-of-the-roost and you'll still see tonkin poles used in larger citizens' races. But tonkin was unhorsed at the 1968 Winter Olympics by aluminum alloy poles, made by Scott of the United States. Scott poles were used in those Olympic races in Autrans, France, by almost all racers not bound by pool agreements to use their own country's products when racing. This meant that it was mostly Americans, Canadians, and Russians who raced with Scotts, while others only envied them. Some Russian racers used their Scotts for as long as six years thereafter in international racing.

Fiberglass shafts had been on and off stage for years, but never in the limelight. Then, in the 1976 Winter Olympics, carbon fiber leapt into prominence when they were used by the overwhelming majority of the medalists.

Now you will find shafts of aluminum alloy, fiberglass, carbon fiber and boron fiber. As with skis, the inherent properties of these materials do not automatically assure pole quality. The skill of the pole maker is still primary.

Aluminum alloy can be made as light and as stiff as other types, provided high quality (and therefore expensive) alloys are used as raw materials. Lower-quality alloys are cheaper, but shafts can bend in use and retain that bend.

Fiberglass shafts are a good compromise between price and performance. Carefully made, they are just a bit heavier than other types, but considerably less expensive. Quality fiberglass shafts have crossing fiber layers. The first is lengthwise along the shaft tube, the second is wound around, the third is lengthwise, and so on, to build up the tubing wall.

Carbon fiber shafts are currently the most popular for high-quality racing poles. Carbon fibers are stronger and stiffer than fiberglass, which means that carbon fiber poles are currently the lightest on the market. (Actually, the term *carbon-fiber shaft/pole* is a slight misnomer, as the shafts are built up of successive layers of carbon fiber and fiberglass strands. The fiberglass is used for the layers wound around the tube, because the stiffer carbon fibers are more brittle, and cannot be bent in small circles.) The chief disadvantage of carbon fiber shafts, other than their high price, is that although strong in skiing use, they can easily be damaged in transport, storage, or handling. A few small transverse scratches, such as those from the metal edges of a ski binding (when poles and skis are tossed into the same bag), is enough to start a fracture line that will cause a pole to break in use. Off snow, carbon fiber poles must be carefully treated. Many racers wrap or bag their poles separately for just this reason.

Boron fiber shafts are the newest on the scene; they were first used in production poles in the 1981-82 season. Like carbon fibers, boron fibers were originally developed for aerospace applications, and accordingly are expensive. On a weight basis, they are stronger than carbon fibers, so theoretically their use can result in lighter shafts. However, as the weight of matrix material, such as epoxy or polyester, that holds the fibers together and gives the shaft its shape is half or more of the final shaft weight, minor reductions in fiber weights are marginal at best. As with skis, it is the skill and quality control in the shaft making process, and not the particular type of exotic fiber used, that determines overall quality.

Shaft profiles may be cylindrical or tapered. Cylindrical shafts are the same diameter throughout their length. They are less expensive because they are simply cut from long lengths of shaft tubing. Tapered shafts give better pole balance and lower pole weight, but are more expensive because they must be made individually.

CLOTHING

As is the case in everyday life, nothing in your collection of gear is more faddish or subject to change than the apparel. Go back a few years to books and magazines published then, and you can read very sound advice on racing. Techniques have changed only negligibly and the basic human body hasn't evolved at all since that time. And snow is still snow. Races and the regulations under which they are run are the same. What will date the material of just a few years ago is the clothing worn by the skiers.

Whether or not to be fashionable is purely a matter of personal choice. Before discussing what is important in the nitty-gritty of good racing togs, we inject one cautionary remark: The clothing worn by top international classified racers is the one part of their gear least useful as a guideline in outfitting yourself for citizens' racing. Remember, in the races where these skiers compete, they are coddled. Coaches and service personnel are at the start and finish. International regulations dictate a minimum standard for wardrobes, waxing rooms, and the like. Teammates and team service personnel man feeding stations. The race organizers literally line the track with timing stations, feeding stations, first aid crews, and track maintenance personnel. If a racer gets in trouble, any trouble, help is right at hand, or at least not far away. But out on the course of a citizens' race, you're on your own. Most organizers man feeding and first aid stations for citizens' races, but it's up to you to find your own warm-ups when you finish, or to shuck them before you start. Lose your cap underway and you may find it at the finish, but then you may not. And so on. In other words, if you emulate the classified racers' dress, you may be underdressing.

If you could spy on the top racers when they're training, you might recognize them by their faces and by their high skiing speeds, but not by their dress. If it's really cold, they bundle up with old team warm-up jackets, loose-fitting track overpants, scarves, odd hats, bicycle shirts, and knitted sweaters. Most of them are neat and efficient, yet a far cry from the way they look on race day.

Your First Line of Defense

Your body is pretty efficient in dealing with cold, but it has limits. Even Eskimos have only partially adapted. Most of their ability to withstand cold comes from their knowledge of how to insulate themselves.

Knowing how your body regulates its heating system is useful in selecting clothing. The body loses heat, mostly through the skin, by convection, evaporation, conduction, and radiation. In most skiing situations, the greatest loss is by convection: the removal of heat by the surrounding air. To cut convection heat loss, avoid moving the surrounding air; trapped air insulates.

Heat loss by evaporation can be almost as great as that by convection. Evaporation cools because heat is required to vaporize water. The evaporation of moisture from the skin through sweat, and from the respiratory tract, account for a fifth or more of heat loss in cold weather. Keep the skin dry to cut evaporation loss.

Conduction loss, the transfer of heat by direct contact, is minimal for most skiing situations. Exceptions are the soles of your feet and the palms of your hands, which are pressed against objects in direct contact with the cold world outside. More insulation is the way to cut conduction loss.

It is not necessary to be fashionable to take part in citizens' races. (Joan Eaton photo)

Radiation loss is negligible for most skiing situations. But on a clear day, the sun heats you by radiation. It supplies energy at a rate of as much as three times your basic rest metabolic power.

It does not take much cold weather experience to learn that the extremities play a major role in the way your body controls its heat reserves. The extremities lose heat easily because they have relatively large surfaces and small volumes. This is why mittens are warmer than gloves. In holding four fingers together and wrapping them in a single insulating shell, you have done nothing to their volume (your hand is still your hand), but you have cut the total exposed surface considerably.

As extremities lose heat, the body reacts to conserve heat. It contracts the blood vessels and constricts the pores in the skin. This restriction has a flywheel effect in cooling the extremities. Blood flow is down, so not as much heat is supplied. But the blood supply is also cooled by the loss of heat to the blood returning from the extremities. This is why the hands and feet become chilled so rapidly in cold weather.

Many racers heed this experience and wear warm gloves or mittens. But even those sensible racers sometimes neglect their feet, thinking that chilly toes are part of the game. That's an error. Chilled extremities can have undesirable effects besides discomfort. Remember, your feet comprise about 10 percent of your body area, and account for 7 to 13 percent of your body heat loss.

The head is unique in the body temperature regulation picture. For normal adults, the head comprises only about 5 percent of the body surface area, yet it releases from 7 to as much as 50 percent of the total body heat loss. This is primarily because the blood supply to the brain is fairly constant. It is not regulated as is the supply to the hands and feet. Also, because of the skull, the blood supply and return paths of the head are relatively near the surface. Finally, the head isn't insulated by a fat layer, as are other parts

Standing, touring, and racing involve increasing energy consumptions.

of the body. These are the facts behind the old saying that, "If you want to keep your feet warm, wear a cap."

Think of what most skiers do when they begin to overheat: they open a collar, unzip or take off a blouse or jacket. This is equivalent to locking the barn door after the horse has been stolen. The better approach is to roll up or peel off a cap before the torso gets uncomfortably warm. This is the basis of the multi-cap trick many racers use to keep warm during a race. They start with two layers on the head, such as a knit wool headband topped by a full knit wool cap. If they start to overheat, they whip off the top cap and stuff it into a pocket. Warmer yet, and they whip off the headband. They reverse the procedure as they cool down.

Clothe as Needed

When you're training or cross-country skiing for pleasure, you can follow the old mountaineering maxim: Suit dress to activity or activity to dress in cold weather so you avoid sweating.

But that won't work in racing because you always overheat and sweat. It's unavoidable. And it poses conflicting requirements for clothing. Racing clothes have to keep you warm, yet allow your body to dump heat so you don't ski along in a sauna of your own sweat. The answer is in layering.

Before you get too warm, peel off some clothing. You can tie an unneeded jacket or sweater around your waist. (John Caldwell photo)

Inner layers act to keep the skin dry and provide some insulation. Therefore, they should transport moisture away from your body and trap some still air. Ideal for this purpose is knitted moisture-transport underwear, usually of a polypropylene blend. These garments absorb little moisture in their fibers, but transport it away from the body. For extra warmth, you can top the garments with thin wool underwear.

Outer layers function mostly to insulate and provide protection against the elements. They also should allow moisture to escape. Two classes of outer layer garments are on the market: (1) two-piece suits, usually knickers and a jacket or blouse, worn with knee socks, and (2) one-piece suits.

Two-piece suits are really great all-arounds. Combined with knicker socks, they allow you the maximum flexibility in dress. If you want to have only one set of duds for skiing, pick a good two-piece suit. Look at the varieties with bib knickers because they have the advantage of keeping the small of your back covered if the blouse rides up. Granted, they aren't as flashy as the one-piece jobs, but you just can't beat their utility. Besides, if your body shape deviates from the norm, you can probably find the best fit in a two-piecer, by purchasing the knickers in one size and the blouse and jacket in another size. One last plus: the knickers are great for summer hiking.

Successive layers are the best dress for racing. (Fletcher Manley photos)

One-piece suits are now the norm in racing. They are available in knee- and ankle-length models. The ankle-length is what the national teams use. The argument for ankle-length models is that they eliminate the sock-to-suit bulge at the knee. At the same time they repel snow, where as knitted socks pick it up.

There are two disadvantages to ankle-length one-piecers, however. First, it's difficult to get a good fit, because you must find one garment that fits your legs, torso, and arms. Second, they're more expensive than other suits. If you're on a budget, you're better off putting more money into better poles, boots, or whatever. Also, one-piece suits make answering calls of nature a major operation. This is no laughing matter when the mercury has dropped out of sight, and it's only minutes to the start of a race. To make matters worse, the current trend in one-piece suits is toward lighter fabrics that make racers look as if they are nude, with color sprayed on. These lighter fabrics do not insulate as well, which means colder extremities.

Remember the Outposts

When recreational skiers take up citizens' racing and buy clothing for it, they usually start with a racing suit, and then add other items later. Our advice is to turn that order around. If you have decent recreational skiing clothes and want to pick up a few garments for racing, start with the extremities: head, hands, and feet.

- **Head.** The two-layer cap trick we mentioned earlier is a good start. Both layers should be good quality thin knits, to allow moisture to escape. For racing or training in extremely cold conditions, you may want to add a pair of earmuffs.

- **Hands.** Gloves or mittens are a must even in warm weather. They protect against pole grip and chafing. Ordinary recreational skiing mittens or gloves and even some work gloves, are fine for lower temperatures. But for racing at temperatures above freezing, you may feel your hands becoming uncomfortably warm. For these conditions, you'll probably want a pair of thin racing gloves with perforated backs that let moisture escape (they're also great biking gloves).

- **Feet.** Ever since the newer, thinner-soled boots arrived, overboots have been a must. There are two basic varieties: insulated overboots for cold weather and waterproof overboots for skiing in slop. Pick the variety that suits the weather where you ski. You may need both, especially if you live in New England, where the weather can go through three seasons in a single week in January.

Some Additional Comforts

There are assorted features of garments that make racing more comfortable. We think that most of this clothing is pretty useful stuff. We use it both on skis and off.

Warm-up suits are great for traveling to races, waxing outdoors when you must, standing around, or warming up before a start. These two-piece suits are usually made of nylon-knit fabric or poplin. They are lined, often with

Pre-start warm-up suits can be many things. (Rune Bergstrom photo)

terry cloth, to absorb sweat. The pants are fitted with full-length zippers on the outside of each leg, so you can put them on or take them off while standing on your skis. Look only at suits with this feature. If you don't have it, the first struggle through the skis off–pants off–skis on routine will make you wish you did. Accept only zippers that go from top to bottom. They're easy to use, hooking on top, and zipping downward with one sweep of the hand along a straight leg. They also allow you to unzip at the ankle to adjust socks or boots, or put on overboots. Avoid zippers that operate from the bottom to the top because they're almost impossible to use. And avoid warm-up pants with fastener tapes in place of a zipper. Fastener tapes are great on shorter stretches when there is a firm backing to press it against, but it is not practical for closing a flapping pant leg together with cold fingers.

Wind jackets or shells are good extra protection whenever you train or race in windy conditions. Most models are light enough so you can whip them off and tie them around your waist if the wind dies down.

Windproof layers on the fronts of racing suits or knickers offer extra protection if you regularly race in windy conditions.

Wind briefs, worn just under or over the first inner layer of underwear, feature windproof cloth fronts to protect the lower abdomen and genitals from wind chill. We use and recommend these briefs for all skiing. Even a speedy downhill in otherwise still conditions can chill the crotch.

Down vests are great for serious warm-ups. They can even be used in cold weather races. After a race when you've changed, they are wonderful for standing around inside awaiting the results. Buildings used for that purpose often seem to be inadequately heated.

RACE ORGANIZATION

If you really get into citizens' racing, sooner or later you may find yourself helping to organize a race. The details involved in this undertaking are numerous and have already been well covered in other material; for further information on most or all of the following general guidelines, refer to the publications listed in #25 below.

1. Attend, or compete in, a few races. Keep track of what features make one race better than another.

2. Start a file. Include entry forms, press releases, and course maps and profiles from other races.

3. Find a sponsor. Good choices are local banks and businesses, insurance companies, ski-equipment manufacturers, and any businesses that might gain from people being healthy. Be prepared to give them press coverage, use bibs and banners with their imprint, and so on.

4. Choose a trail and request landowners' permissions to use it. If prevailing law would hold them responsible for the racers who are using the property, give them a properly executed waiver.

5. Get adequate insurance. You'll need coverage not only for the race but also for whenever the trail is open for practice. Also have a waiver printed on the back of the entry form for each racer to sign.

6. Groom the trail in the off-season.

7. Get a post office box for race business. Questions prior to the race are endless; no one person wants to receive all that mail—or the phone calls.

8. Determine entry fees. They should cover costs of printing, stationery, postage, secretarial help, racing bibs, refreshments for racers, insurance, paid professional help, parking lot rental, and maintenance work.

9. Order paper racing bibs.

10. Order prizes. We don't believe in elaborate prizes—just certificates, or trophies that are engraved and passed on each year.

11. Mail entry blanks three weeks before the race.

12. Prepare recorder cards as entry blanks come in. On race day, having these cards filled out with racer information will speed up getting race results to the skiers.

13. Notify local authorities.

14. Arrange for toilet facilities. Look under "Toilets, portable" in the Yellow Pages to acquire the bare necessities, which must be available at the race site.

15. Set up parking facilities. If the race begins and ends in different locations shuttles will then be necessary to transport skiers back to the start.

16. Arrange for medical assistance. Most areas have rescue groups or Nordic patrols who can help; at smaller races, it might suffice to have some doctors on call. After any race, be sure to conduct a trail sweep to pick up

any racers or spectators who might have had some difficulty on the tracks.

17. Get experienced people to handle public relations. This is particularly important for large races.

18. Prepare the tracks.

19. Choose timers who are good with numbers. They can use one of several race-timing methods and race starts.

20. Use lots of signs. Be sure parking facilities, race headquarters, toilet facilities, the course itself, and so on are clearly marked.

21. Post wax and temperature information. Find a coach or experienced racer who can suggest wax for race day. Also post air and snow temperatures that have been taken along the course.

22. Provide race refreshments (see "Liquid Thoughts" in "The Inner Racer").

23. Record finish times.

24. Clean up after the race. It also doesn't hurt to go by after the snow has melted in order to pick up anything that the earlier cleanup crews might have missed. Don't forget to thank the landowner.

25. For further information, consult the following:
    - "Recommended Reading"
    - *FIS Rulebook*. Available from the United States Ski Association at Olympic Training Center, Colorado Springs, Colorado 80909, or P.O. Box 100, Park City, Utah 84060; or from the Canadian Ski Association, 333 River Road, Ottawa, Ontario K1L 8B9.
    - United States Ski Association or Canadian Ski Association rules for cross-country competitions. Available from the USSA and CSA addresses.
    - *An Organizer's Manual for Cross-Country Citizen Racing*. Available from the USSA address.
    - *Cross-Country Ski Trail and Facility Design Manual*. A loose-leaf manual published by the Ontario Ski Council, 160 Vanderhoof Avenue, Toronto, Ontario M4G 4B8.

SKI ASSOCIATIONS AND RACES

Some useful addresses follow. For more information, contact your ski association headquarters.

U.S. Ski Association
P.O. Box 100
Park City, Utah 84060
(801) 649-6935

Olympic Training Center
Colorado Springs, Colorado 80909

The USSA is organized into eight geographical divisions. Check with your local club or ski shop, or contact USSA for further information.

Canadian Ski Association
333 River Road
Vanier, Ontario K1L 8B9
(613) 746-0000

The CSA is organized into member associations in the provinces. Check with your local club or ski shop, or contact CSA headquarters for further information.

U.S. Ski Coaches Association
P.O. Box 1747
Park City, Utah 84000
(801) 649-9090

World Loppet
Telemark Lodge
Cable, Wisconsin 54821
(715) 798-3811

Great American Ski Chase
USSA
P.O. Box 727
Brattleboro, Vermont 05301
(802) 257-7113

RECOMMENDED READING

We use these references, and recommend them to those who wish to dig deeper into the various aspects of citizens' racing. All are in English and available in North America.

BIOMECHANICS

Ekström, Hans. *Biomechanical Research Applied to Skiing*. Linköping, Sweden: Linköping Studies in Science and Technology, 1980.

A thorough modern study; perhaps a future classic.

Miller, Doris I., and Nelson, Richard C. *Biomechanics of Sport*. Philadelphia: Lea & Febiger, 1976.

An excellent text overview of the field.

PHYSIOLOGY

Åstrand, Per-Olaf, and Rodahl, Kaare. *Textbook of Work Physiology: Physiological Basis of Exercisers*. 2nd ed. New York: McGraw-Hill, 1977.

The acknowledged Bible of the subject.

Bergh, Ulf. *The Physiology of Cross-Country Ski Racing*. Translated by Michael Brady and Marianne Hadler. Champaign, Illinois: Human Kinetics Publishers, 1981.

The standard reference on cross-country ski racing physiology.

Mellerowicz, Harald. *Ergometry: Basics of Medical Exercise Testing*. Edited by Vojin N. Smodlaka. Baltimore: Urban & Schwarzenberg, 1981.

The complete guide to measuring human performance.

Silverstein, Alvin. *Human Anatomy & Physiology*. New York: John Wiley, 1980.

Superb text explanations, beautifully illustrated in color.

FITNESS PHYSIOLOGY AND SPORTSMEDICINE

Hixon, Edward G. *The Physicians & Sportsmedicine Guide to Cross-Country Skiing*. New York: McGraw-Hill, 1980.

A U.S. Ski Team doctor's approach to the sport.

Jerome, John. *The Sweet Spot in Time.* New York: Summit Books, 1980.

How perfection in sport is attained and what it feels like to achieve it in almost all the sports currently practiced in North America; recommended reading for all competitors.

Sharkey, Brian J. *Physiology of Fitness.* Champaign, Illinois: Human Kinetics Publishers, 1979.

A thorough overview; the inside story of fitness.

MEDICINE

Ward, Michael. *Mountain Medicine.* London: Crosby Lockwood Staples, 1975.

A storehouse of information by a recognized authority.

Wilkerson, James A. *Medicine for Mountaineering.* 2nd ed. Seattle: The Mountaineers, 1978.

Written for wilderness and expedition travel but full of information for all cold-weather performance situations.

RACING

Caldwell, John. *Caldwell on Competitive Cross-Country Skiing.* Brattleboro, Vermont: Stephen Greene Press, 1979.

An all-around guide to cross-country ski competition.

Lier, Hal, and Peterson, Howard. *I Hope I Get a Purple Ribbon.* Brattleboro, Vermont: U.S. Ski Association, 1980.

A straightforward guide on how to get kids into racing.

EQUIPMENT

Brady, Michael. *Cross-Country Ski Gear.* Seattle: The Mountaineers, 1979.

The most complete book reference on the subject.

WAXING

Brady, Michael, and Skjemstad, Lorns. *Waxing for Cross-Country Skiing.* 6th ed. Berkeley: Wilderness Press, 1981.

A small booklet that covers the subject, from recreation through racing.

TRAILS

Ontario Ski Council. *Cross-Country Ski Trail and Facility Design Manual*. Toronto: Ontario Ski Council, 1980.

The most complete and comprehensive handbook available on trail design, maintenance, and preparation.

CROSS-COUNTRY SKIING—GENERAL

Brady, Michael. *Nordic Touring & Cross Country Skiing*. 5th ed. Oslo & Baltimore: Dreyers, 1979.

A standby of the sport, first published in the mid-1960s.

Brady, Michael. *Ski Cross-Country*. 2nd ed. New York: Dial Press, 1982.

A comprehensive overview.

Caldwell, John. *The Cross-Country Ski Book*. 6th ed. Brattleboro, Vermont: Stephen Greene Press, 1981.

Another standby of the sport, first published in the mid-1960s.

Gillette, Ned. *Cross-Country Skiing*. Seattle: The Mountaineers, 1979.

Cross-country skiing's renaissance man speaks with authority on the subject; includes chapters on adventure skiing.

GLOSSARY

Cross-country ski racing has its own special vocabulary that describes the activity and its gear. Here are the most commonly used terms. Definitions or applications that don't pertain directly to cross-country skiing are not given. All trade names and trademarks are assumed registered.

ABS: Plastic used in skis and bindings.
Acrylic: (1) Foam plastic used in ski cores. (2) Fibers or fabric, used in clothing.
Active surface: Portion of ski base actively in contact with snow; usually denotes the contact length, but sometimes only the midsection of base waxed for grip, or containing waxless base pattern.
Aerobic: Literally "with air"; describes body processes that require oxygen.
Aerobic capacity: A measure of the ability to perform aerobic work over longer periods of time. Often expressed as maximum oxygen uptake.
Alpine skiing: Recreational and competitive downhill skiing, developed in Europe's Alps in the 1920s.
Anaerobic: Literally "without air"; describes body processes that can function without oxygen. Sometimes termed *oxygen debt*.
Anaerobic capacity: A measure of the body's capability to perform muscular work over and above the limit set by maximum oxygen uptake.
Aramid: Synthetic fiber used in structural layers of skis.
Arm trainers: Various devices used by ski racers in off-season arm training; provide resistance against arms in poling movements.
Arterio-venous oxygen difference (a-vO_2): Difference in oxygen content of blood pumped by heart through arteries to tissues and that of blood returned by veins to heart.

Backslip: Skis grip snow poorly and slip backward.
Bail: Clamp-down piece on toe binding; holds boot sole down with or against pins.
Base: (1) Running surface of a ski. (2) Snow under surface snow.
Base preparation: Compounds or process of their application to plastic ski bases.
Base wax: Wax used "under" final wax to increase durability.
Basket: Disk attached near bottom of ski pole to prevent its sinking into snow.
Biathlon: Competitive skiing event combining cross-country ski racing and rifle marksmanship.
Biomechanics: The study of human motion.
Boat: Ski side profile, waist broader than tip or tail.
Bowed: Ski base convex instead of flat, center higher than edges.
Box: Synthetic ski construction in which load-carrying material forms a box enclosing core on all four sides.

Calorie: Thermal unit, the amount of heat required at a pressure of one atmosphere to raise the temperature of 1 gr of water 1°C.

Camber: Arch of the middle of a ski above its tip and tail.
Camber pocket: Horizontal length under portion of camber curve not yet flattened out when ski is weighted.
Camber resistance: Force necessary to flatten out a ski's camber.
Camber stiffness: Stiffness distributed over ski's camber, uniformly or nonuniformly, usually expressed as force required to straighten out portion of camber in question.
Carbon fiber: Filaments of carbon, used in ski poles and structural layers of skis, usually encased in epoxy resin.
Cardiac output: Volume of blood that heart pumps per minute.
Citizens' race: Cross-country ski race for recreational skiers, usually mass start; the subject of this book.
Clog: To collect snow and ice up, said of ski bases.
Combined: In Nordic skiing, competition combining 15-km cross-country ski racing and ski jumping on a 70-m hill.
Conduction: Transfer of heat by direct contact.
Contact length: Length of ski base in contact with underlying surface when ski is not weighted.
Convection: Transfer of heat through circulation of air.
Core: Central part of wood or synthetic ski, between or encased by structural layers; gives ski shape.
Cork: A block of material, originally natural cork, now usually foam plastic, used to rub and polish ski wax on ski base.
Corn: Large-grained snow, produced by settling and repeated freezing and thawing.
Cosmetics: External color, design, logos, lettering, and so on, especially on skis, boots, and poles.
Course: Route followed by a ski race.
Cross-country: In common usage, the entirety of recreational ski touring and competitive cross-country ski racing.
Crust: Glazed snow surface, caused by freeze-thaw cycles.

Deconditioning: The reverse of conditioning; the gradual loss of training effect after training ceases.
Diagonal stride: Stride in which opposite arm and leg move in unison, as in walking on foot.
Distance training: Endurance training, used by racers, aimed at building aerobic power.
Double camber: Geometric interpretation of modern ski camber where center section is stiffer than tip or tail sections.
Double-poling: Gliding ski maneuver in which both arms move in unison, planting poles for forward thrust.
Dry-snow skis: Racing skis for use on dry snow, usually with relatively softer camber stiffness and high-density plastic base.
Dynamic: In motion. Usually an adjective, such as *dynamic force*, a force due to motion.

Edge: Bottom outside edge of ski base, of material differing from rest of base.
Egg: Ultracompact, crouching downhill ski position.

Electric waxer: Electrically heated waxing iron, usually with a reservoir for melted wax and a mechanism for dispensing wax directly onto ski base.
Endurance: The time limit of a person's ability to perform.
Epoxy: A resin, used as an adhesive and as a binder for various synthetic fibers in skis and poles.
Evaporation: Process of converting water to vapor; requires heat.
Evaporative ability: Ability of a wet clothing fiber to allow moisture evaporation.

Fall line: Shortest line directly down a hill.
Fartslek: From the Swedish; literally "speed game," a form of off-snow training for racing.
Fiberglass: Glass filaments, spun or thrown together, then encased in a resin, often epoxy, to form structural layers of skis and ski pole shafts.
FIS: Fédèration Internationale de Ski—The International Ski Federation.
Flex: Bending properties of a ski or ski pole.
Flexibility: (1) Flex. (2) Measure of physical movement capability, such as how far a body part can bend.
Friction: Resistance between two surfaces that are sliding over one another; when surfaces slide, friction produces heat.

Gaiter: Cloth covering around leg and boot at ankle; keeps out snow.
Glide: Property of a ski base that allows it to slide on snow.
Glider: Paraffin wax used on tip and tail section of ski bases for glide.
Going under: Debilitation, usually synonymous with exhaustion.
Granular snow: Snow comprised of large, coarse crystals.
Grip: (1) Property of a ski that allows it to bite into underlying snow. (2) The handle of a ski pole.
Groove: (1) Long, narrow indentation in ski base; aids tracking. (2) Indentation, often V-shaped, in bottom surface of boot heel; mates with device on ski. (3) Round indentation around outside of boot heel, to hold cable of cable-type binding.

Hard wax: Wax for cold and dry to slightly wet snow.
Heel plate: Plate mounted on ski under boot heel, usually with features designed to hold weighted heel on ski.
Herringbone: Uphill stride, skis spread to form a V; named for pattern left in snow.
Hydrophilic: Having a strong affinity for water (attracting or absorbing water). Used to describe materials.
Hydrophobic: Having little or no affinity for water (repelling water). Used to describe materials.
Hyperventilation: Breathing technique used to take in more air than normal.
Hypothermia: Subnormal body temperature that slows physiological processes and can result in death.

Imitation training: Movements performed on foot to imitate and thus teach skiing movements.
Imprinted length: Length stamped or printed on skis or poles.

Interval training: A series of intense, short exercise periods separated by rests. Used by racers in off-season training.
IOC: The International Olympic Committee.

Kick: As in walking, a backward thrusting toe push-off and leg extension that provides forward thrust in skiing strides.
Kicker: Grip wax applied in midsection of ski base.
Kick turn: A stationary about-face turn performed by lifting and reversing the direction of one ski, followed by the other ski.
Klister: Tacky, fluid cross-country wax preparations, for wet and/or settled snow.
Klister ski: Competition ski specifically designed for use on wet snow, with klister.
Klister-wax: Tacky, hard wax for conditions near freezing.
Knickers: Breeches gathered at the knee, usually with elastic or buckle strap.

Lighted track: Illuminated cross-country trail or track.

Muscular fitness: Ability of the skeletal muscles to perform movements.

Negative base: Pattern-type waxless ski base where waxless pattern lies under level of base.
Nordic: (1) Geographic: Norway, Sweden, and Finland. (2) Recreational and competitive cross-country skiing, biathlon, ski jumping equipment and apparel.
Nordic Norm: Standard boot and toe binding widths and side angles, most common (1979–80) for recreational cross-country boots and bindings.
Norm 38: Design of racing boots and bindings, patented and developed in Central Europe.
Nylon: Originally trade name but now accepted as generic term for type of polyamide plastic, used in parts of skis, poles, boots, and bindings, and in fiber form, in ski apparel.

Overboots: Flexible, pull-over boot covers, for added insulation and water repellency.
Overdistance: Distance training for racing, usually off-season on foot, over distance greater than competitive racing distance.
Oxygen debt: Anaerobic.
Oxygen uptake: Measure of a body's ability to consume oxygen.

Parallel turn: Downhill turn made with skis parallel throughout turn.
Pattern base: Waxless ski base where irregularities that grip comprise a regular pattern molded or machined into base material.
Peaking: Time during racing season when racer produces optimum results.
Physiology: For skiing purposes, usually work physiology, the study of body processes involved in human performance.
Pin: (1) Short peg projecting upward from base plate of toe binding; engages recess in boot sole. (2) Transverse spike that holds grip on ski pole.
Pin binding: Toe binding comprised of metal or plastic toepiece with pins projecting upward to mate with recesses in boot sole.
Pole set: The act of planting a pole in the snow.

Poling: Arm movements with poles that supply forward thrust.
Polyethylene (PE): Plastic derived from ethylene gas, used for ski bases.
Polypropylene (PP): Plastic derived from propane gas, used for ski bases; fibers used in fabrics for transport-type underwear.
Polyurethane (PU): Gray or black foam plastic, used for boot soles and ski cores, especially of injected type. Fiber used in stretch fabrics.
Positive base: Pattern-type waxless ski base where waxless pattern protrudes beyond the level of the base.
Powder: Light, dry snow, usually at low temperatures.
Pulk: Kayak-shaped sled, riding directly on snow as does toboggan, used by skiers to transport loads, small children, or injured.

Racing Norm: Standard for racing boots and bindings.
Radiation: Direct heat transfer through space; example is process whereby sun warms body.
Railed: Ski base concave instead of flat, edges higher than center.
Relay: In cross-country ski racing, a four-man, 40-km race or a four-woman, 20-km race. Shorter relays or mixed men's and women's are run nationally in some countries.
Resilience: (1) Ski or pole spring. (2) Part of muscular fitness.
Roller skis: Skatelike platforms that attach like skis to boots, for simulating ski movements, off-season, in training for racing.
Rucksack: Knapsack with a frame, suitable for skiing.

Sandwich ski: Wood or synthetic ski built up of several laminations bonded together in a sandwichlike fashion.
Scraper: Metal or plastic rectangle or blade, used to remove old wax or flatten bases.
Shaft: Tubular, straight part of a ski pole.
Shank: Reinforcing insert in boot sole, usually under arch of foot.
Shovel: Upturned part of a ski tip.
Side camber: Sidecut.
Sidecut: Concave curve on side profile of a ski that gives it slight hourglass shape; aids tracking and helps banked ski turn.
Sideslip: Skis gliding sideways under control.
Side walls: Sides of a ski, usually of hard material to protect more fragile core.
Skating turn: Flat terrain or downhill turn; executed by one or more skating steps in new direction.
Ski-striding: A variation of walking or running, done uphill on foot to imitate skiing movements.
Ski tester: Device for measuring camber stiffness, usually with electric indicators and mechanism to produce and indicate force applied.
Ski touring: Recreational cross-country skiing, usually in wilderness.
Snowmobile: Tracked motorized vehicle for travel on snow, usually with runners for steering; useful for supply transport, rescue, and pulling track setters. Recreational use curtailed or forbidden in most countries, but permitted in United States and Canada.
Snowplow: Downhill position for slowing down, stopping, and turning ski tips together, tails apart.

Snowplow turn: Downhill turn executed in the snowplow position.
Specificity: Training or exercises that relate directly to a specific skiing maneuver or event.
Speed training: Physical training aimed at attaining high speed in racing.
Static: At a standstill. Usually an adjective, as in *weight is a static force.*
Stem turn: Downhill turn in which one ski is angled out, pointing in the new direction, to initiate the turn.
Step: (1) Stepped turn. (2) Sawtoothlike pattern embossed on waxless ski base.
Strength: (1) Usually breaking strength, force required to fracture ski or pole. (2) A component of muscular fitness—the force that can be exerted in a specific movement.
Stride: The walklike movements that propel a skier forward.
Stroke volume: Volume of blood pumped per heartbeat by a single ventricle.
Structural layer: Layers of a ski that carry most of the loads.
Synthetic fabrics: Fabrics woven or knitted from yarns spun or thrown from synthetic fiber filaments.
Synthetic skis: Skis in which the structural layers are made of synthetic materials, such as fiber-plastic laminations or metal.

Tail: The rear end of a ski.
Telemark: (1) Region in south-central Norway. (2) Skiing position originated in Telemark—both knees bent, one leg trailing the other.
Telemark turn: A steered downhill ski turn, one of the oldest known, named for region in Norway. Characterized by little or no sideslip of skis, body in Telemark position, arms spread wide for balance.
Tempo training: Running or skiing at racing speed for periods of 10 to 20 percent of a race's duration.
Tip: (1) Front end of a ski. (2) Bottom end of ski pole.
Toe binding: Bindings that attach boots to skis by clamping front part of sole welt.
Top sheet: (1) Upper surface sheet of synthetic ski, usually with ski cosmetics. (2) Top grain leather.
Touring: (1) Cross-country skiing. (2) Heavier cross-country ski equipment, intended for wilderness use.
Touring Norm: Standard for boots and bindings, using Racing Norm profiles and Nordic Norm boot sole thicknesses.
Track: (1) Path a skier has taken. (2) Prepared tracks for cross-country skiing. (3) Shouted warning, used by racer in overtaking another skier.
Tracking: Ability of ski or pulk to follow straight course.
Track setter: Sled used to prepare ski trails and set tracks in snow, usually pulled by a snowmobile.
Training: Any physical activity that maintains or improves physical ability.
Transition snow: Snow just at freezing, in transition zone between dry and wet.
Transport-type underwear: Underwear of fabric that keeps skin dry by transporting moisture out, away from the body.
Traversing: Skiing up or down a hill on a traverse at an angle to the fall line.

Velcro: Trade name for nylon closure tape, in pairs, one of which consists of loops, the other of pile; tapes lock to each other with slight pressure and are opened by a firm pull.

Warm-down: The reverse of warm-up; done after exercise.

Warm-up: Exercise of gradually increasing intensity; done before training or racing, to help bring body processes up to optimum functioning.

Waxable skis: Skis whose bases are waxed for grip and glide.

Waxing iron: Iron for waxing; may be heated by flame or electricity.

Wax torch: Small blowtorch, usually fueled by liquefied gas, used in waxing skis.

Waxless ski: Ski with irregularity in base that both grips and glides on snow without wax.

Wax remover: Solvent used to remove wax from ski bases.

Wax zone: Areas on ski bases where grip waxes should be applied.

Weight shift: The transfer of weight from one ski to the other. In ski strides, as in walking or running, transfer also involves dynamic (due to motion) forces in addition to body weight, so *weight shift* is strictly speaking a misleading term.

Wet-snow skis: Racing skis for use on wet snow, usually with relatively stiffer cambers, often with softer, lower-density plastic bases.

Wide-track: Stance in downhill skiing, skis parallel and 4 to 12 in. apart.

Wind chill: Loss of insulating effect of air surrounding the body as wind increases.

Wood skis: Skis in which the structural layers are of wood.

World Cup: International cross-country racing competiton for men and women racers. Points are awarded for a racer's best five results in nine preselected races each season. The skier with the most points at the end of the season is the World Cup winner.

World Loppet: League of ten major international citizens' races, one in Canada, one in the U.S., three in Scandinavia, and five in Central Europe.

Wrist strap: Strap fastened to ski pole grip, fits around wrist to prevent pole loss.

WSC: World Ski Championships, held in even-numbered years between leap years; arranged by the FIS.

XC: Common abbreviation for cross-country.

INDEX

Boldface numerals indicate pages on which photos or illustrations appear.

Ability, 64. *See also* Technique
Aerobic capacity, 66-67, 68, 69
Aerobic training zone, 49-51
Alcoholic beverages, 36, 72
Anaerobic exercise, 48
Anaerobic processes, 68, 69
Arm movements, 76-77, 158, 159
Arterio-venous oxygen difference, 67

Bicycling, 27, 40, **41**, 45, 66
Binders, 120-21, 123
Bindings. *See* Boot-binding systems
Biomechanics, 65, 175
Birkebeiner, 15, 16-**18**, **29**, **150**
Blood capacity, 67
Boot-binding systems, 152-57
   selection of, 156-57
Bounding, 93

Camber, 140-42, 144-45, 146, **147**-48, 150-51
Carbohydrate-loading, 52
Chola, 121, 122
Clothing, 53-54, 162-69
Corks, **127**, 129
Cross-country skiing, 14, 176

Diagonal stride, 65, **75**-76, 79, **80**, 81-82, 85, 86
   uphill, 92-94, 96
Diet, 52-53. *See also* Food; Liquids
Dogtrotting, 94, 96
Double-poling, 78, 80, **84**, **85**-88, 104, 106
Downhill technique, 100-102, **103**
Drafting, 27

Eating, 32-33, 52-53, 72
Egg-position, 77, **101**, 102

Equipment, 14, 25-26, 137-62, 176
   roller skiing, 56-58

First aid, 175-76
Fitness, level of, 49-51, 61, 63, 90, 133. *See also* Training
Food, 28, 32-33, 52-53, 72. *See also* Liquids
Forward drive, 82, 84-85

Glide zone, 115, 136
Going under, 47-48, 52, 68
Grip wax. *See* Waxes, kicker
Grip zone, 113-15

Half herringbone, **99**
Health, general, 61
Heart capacity, 66-67
Herringbone, **38**, 90, 96-**98**, 106
Hills. *See* Uphill technique

Illness, 33, 39, 41,42
Injury, 41-42, 43, 45

Jet lag, 24-25

Kick, 65, 75-76, 79, 81-82, 104. *See also* Diagonal stride
Kicker zone, 113-15, 120

Liquids, 28, 32-33, 36, 52-53, 71-72
Loppets, 10, 14-15
Lung capacity, 66

Medical information, 175-76. *See also* Biomechanics; Fitness; Physiology
Monitoring. *See* Pacing

Negative work, 68

Oxygen debt, 47-48, 90
Oxygen uptake, 67, 69

Pacing, 27, 28, 45-52
Pain, 48
Paper test, 113, **147**
Physiology, 66-68, 175
Poles, 157-62
Pulse rates, 42, 48-51, 52

Races, citizens', 9-10, **12**-33
　courses for, 17, 39, 88
　entering of, 23-24
　finishing times for, 64
　organization of, 171-72
　recovery after, 32-33
　tips for, 13-14, 26-28, 90, 129
　types of, 10, 15-23
　"typical," 28-32
Roller skiing, **55**-**60**, **69**
Rowing, 41
Running, 36, 41, **42**, 45-47, 51-52, 66
　with diagonal stride, 96

Salt, 72
Sanding, 113, 120, 124-26
Scrapers, 107, 124, 126-**27**, 134, 135, 136
Shuffle, 93
Sidecut, 139
Skate, marathon, 88
Skating, 85, 88, **89**, **103**, **105**
Ski association, 173
Skill, 64-65. *See also* Technique
Skis, 25, 109, 133, 138-51
　bases of, 124, 126, 139-40, **149**-50
　cleaning of, 126, 134-36
　dry-snow, 141, 142, **143**
　klister, 141-42, 147, 148
　materials in, 142-43
　new, 113, 124
　powder, 141, 142, 147
　selection of, 144-51
　waxless, 111, 134
　wet-snow, 141-42, **143**
　wood, 113
Ski-striding, **38**, **46-47**, 82
Sneak, 93

Snow, artificial, 132
Snow conditions. *See* Tracks
Snowplow, **100**
Speed-skiing, 64, 65, 74, **77**-78, 79-81
Suction, 118-19, 126
Sugar, 71-72
Swedish Scale for Perceived
　Exertion, 51-52

Technique, 58, 64, 65, 73-110, 133
　different tracks, 102, 103-107
　downhill, 100-102, **103**
　uphill, 89-99
Torches, 123, **125**, 135
Tracks, 79-80, 88, **89**, 90, 102, 104-107
　and camber, 141-42
　preparation of, 128-29
　snow in, 131-32
　wax for, 116-17, 118-19
Training, 33, 35-54, 63, 64, 69, 80-81
　clothing for, 53-54
　equipment for, 35, **44**, **49**, **55**
　programs for, 36, 175, 176
　progressive, 40
　roller skiing, **55**-**60**
　specificity, 35, 40-41
　workouts, 39-40, 42, 54
Travel, 24-25, 123, 134

Uphill technique, 88, 90-**94**, 96-**99**
　slight inclines, 91-92
　steeper hills, 92-94, 96-99

Vasaloppet, 15-**16**, 128

Waxes, 26, 40, 121
　age of, 132-33
　application of, **114**, 115, 119-27, 129, 133, 151
　binders, 120-21, 123
　glide, 115, 117-19, **122**, 123, 136
　hard, **114**, 116, 119, 120-21, 123, 129, 133-34, 135, 136
　kicker, **114**, 115-16, 120, 151
　klister, 106-107, 116-17, 120-21, 129, 134, 136
　removal of, 134-36

186

selection of, 111-13, 115-19, 128,
    132-33
Waxing, 40, 104, 106-107, 111-36, 176
Weight shift, 74, **75**
World Loppet, 18-23, **28**

Michael Brady (left) and John Caldwell.

The Authors

John Caldwell has spent a lifetime racing, coaching, and spreading the word about cross-country skiing and cross-country ski racing. He was the U.S. Ski Team head cross-country coach from 1966 through 1972, and has authored half a dozen books on the sport. He teaches math and skiing at the Putney School, in Putney, Vermont.

Michael Brady is an American living in Oslo, Norway, and is one of the few foreigners certified as a cross-country ski racing coach in that country. Through the late 1960s and mid-1970s, as the Nordic editor for *Ski* Magazine, his articles helped spark the cross-country skiing renaissance. He has written five books on the sport, some of which have been published in four languages.

Together, Caldwell and Brady have a wealth of knowledge of the sport unequaled in North America. They both have raced and coached on three continents: North America, Europe, and Australia. They first thought of writing this book one evening in 1968, after finishing the 85.6-km Vasaloppet citizens' race. It was, they then agreed, a sport that would soon sweep North America. This book is the documentation of that thought.

The skiers who skied for Fletcher Manley's photos of technique in this book are as deeply involved in cross-country racing as are the authors.

Marianne Hadler, who skied for the women's sequences, has coached in Canada and Vermont, and in 1981, the year the photos in this book were taken, won the American Birkebeiner, the Yukon Jack, and several other citizens' races. She is married to author Michael Brady.

Peter Caldwell, who skied for the men's sequences, has been a skier and racer for as long as he can remember. He is now the Nordic ski coach for Vermont Academy. His brother Tim is on the U.S. Nordic Ski Team. He is the son of author John Caldwell.

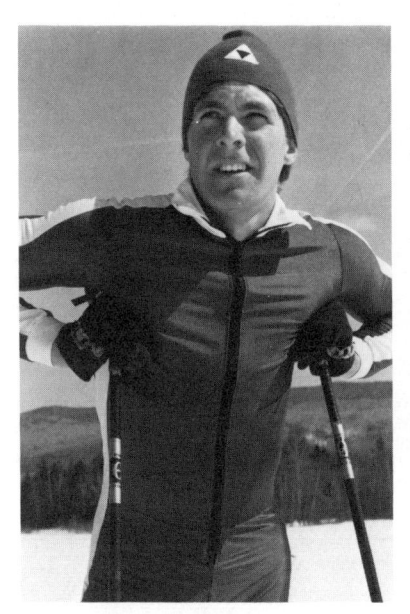

Peter Caldwell (left) and Marianne Hadler.